Sing the Lord's Song in a Strange Land

SPRING
HARVEST
Equipping the Church for action

Also available in Braille and Giant Print

Copyright©2005 Spring Harvest

Gerard Kelly asserts the moral right to be identified as the author of this work.

Published by
Spring Harvest
14 Horsted Square
Uckfield
East Sussex TN22 1QG

First edition 2005

ISBN   1 899 78850 6

Acknowledgements
Unless stated otherwise, all Scripture quotations taken from the HOLY BIBLE, NEW INTERNATIONAL VERSION.
Copyright ©1973, 1978, 1984 by International Bible Society.
Used by permission of Hodder and Stoughton Limited.
All rights reserved. "NIV" is a registered trade mark of International Bible Society.
UK trademark number 1448790

Scripture taken from The Message. Copyright © 1993, 1994, 1995, 1996, 2000, 2001, 2002. Used by permission of NavPress Publishing Group.

Taken from The Street Bible by Rob Lacey. Copyright ©2003 by Rob Lacey. Used by permission of Zondervan.

The author would like to express his thanks to the following, who have all made valuable contributions to the Spring Harvest 2005 Study Guide.
Theological editors: Mary Evans, Stephen Gaukroger, Ernest Lucas
Theme Consultation Day: Doug Balfour, Steve Chalke, Graham Daniels, Joel Edwards, David Firth, Dave Godfrey, Philip Greenslade, Peter Meadows, Ann Morisy, Pete Phillips, Martin Thomas, Viv Thomas, Tony Watkins, Ben Wickham

Please note that the inclusion of a quotation or example in this book does not imply endorsement by Spring Harvest.

Spring Harvest. A Registered Charity.

sing
the Lord's song in a strange land

Spring Harvest 2005

STUDY GUIDE

by Gerard Kelly

SPRING HARVEST

Equipping the Church for action

Daniel: Far from home but not forgotten

"How can we sing the LORD's song in a strange land?"

Psalm 137:4 *(paraphrase)*

Introduction

How can we sing God's song – live God's life and be God's people – in a land in which we are exiles? When all around us changes and the props we have relied on are removed, can we keep the faith?

The psalmist asks the question: In many ways Daniel answers it. The unforgettable stories of this book show what it means to 'sing the songs of the LORD while in a foreign land'; to keep the faith in times of trial and testing.

Rooted in the sixth century before Christ, when the Hebrews were in exile, told and re-told 400 years later, when they were under occupation and the very survival of their nation was threatened, these stories have served for generations of Jewish and Christian believers as a reminder of the faithfulness of God.

We have faith because God is faithful. We sing because God's song will not be silenced.

At Spring Harvest 2005 we are exploring the stories of Daniel and his companions in exile, and asking what lessons we might learn in the changing pressures of our own context and culture.

Our **Four Daily Themes**, shared by all age groups across the Main Event, are:

Day 2
Presence: faith in a foreign land   page 8

Day 3
Prophecy: faith for the future   page 32

Day 4
Pressure: faith in the furnace   page 60

Day 5
Power: faith in a faithful God   page 86

Our **Bible Readings** will work through the first seven chapters of Daniel, following the 'chiastic' structure of the book (a literary form in which the concerns and themes of the early chapters are 'mirrored' in later chapters in a concentric pattern):

Day 2: Daniel 1	The journey into exile
Day 3: Daniel 2 and 7	Two prophetic dreams
Day 4: Daniel 3 and 6	Two miracles of divine deliverance
Day 5: Daniel 4 and 5	Two kings assessed and judged

The **Zones** will develop particular topics from these chapters, taking our theme of 'faith in exile' *from Daniel into contemporary* experience. Each Zone addresses a different area of contemporary life, and each Zone features three teaching blocks through which to explore the issues of the day.

The **Study Guide** is laid out for each day with an introduction to the overall theme and an overview of the Daniel material, followed by three teaching blocks. After each teaching block, there are two discussion starters.

Question Time suggests significant questions for discussion, reflection or further study. These may be used as discussion starters in the Zone, or by individuals and groups using the Study Guide outside the Zone context.

In The Zone homes in on each of the specialist areas covered by the teaching Zones, suggesting key questions to apply the Study Guide to the particular area being covered.

Our **Evening Celebrations** will engage with the theme of exile in the New Testament. Using key passages from the book of Acts, we will learn from Spirit-filled communities living as resident aliens in the Roman Empire.

Day 2

Presence:
Faith in a foreign land

Outline of the Day:

Introduction: Presence
Overview: Daniel 1

Introduction: Presence

The book of Daniel invites us, through a series of stories, to explore the lives of a small group of friends taken by force from Jerusalem to Babylon. The setting for these stories is exile – four young Hebrews are pitted against the nation-crushing might of the Babylonian Empire, the most powerful political force in the known world of their day. The odds are overwhelmingly against them – and yet their presence in Babylon becomes a factor of national significance. For all their powerlessness these exiles, and particularly their spokesman Daniel, are able to make a difference in the hostile culture and context to which they are deported. Like yeast in a batch of dough, like a mustard seed sunk deep into the soil, like a few grains of well-placed salt, the exiles learn to 'keep the faith' in Babylon. These remarkable biblical texts have inspired Jewish and Christian believers for centuries – and they continue to offer lessons for today's church. As we explore these important stories, we will ask:

- What might the 'exile' of Daniel and the Hebrew deportees have to teach us in our own post-Christendom society?

- Is 'living in Babylon' a metaphor we can use and learn from?

- How did Daniel and his friends respond to their loss of power and the seeming defeat of Israel's God?

- What new aspects of God's sovereignty, character and plan were revealed through the trials the exiles faced?

- What strategies did they adopt not only to survive but to thrive in hostile times?

> ### Key verse:
> To these four young men God gave knowledge and understanding of all kinds of literature and learning. And Daniel could understand visions and dreams of all kinds.
> ### Daniel 1:17

Overview: Daniel 1

Daniel 1 introduces us to four young men who have been taken by force from Jerusalem to Babylon. Associated with the higher echelons of Jewish society, these young men are to be re-educated and trained for service in the Babylonian Empire. The chapter sees our heroes making the journey from Jerusalem to Babylon and settling in to their new situation. It describes in detail three key aspects of this exile experience.

1. The extensive programme of education and orientation that these young men were to receive – preparing them for top-level jobs in the Babylonian civil service.

2. The decision by the official in charge of this programme to re-name its participants, giving them names derived from the worship of Babylon and gods.

3. The 'act of resistance' organised by Daniel and undertaken by all four of the group, whereby they choose to fast from the high-quality food brought from the palace kitchen and live instead on vegetables and water. The success of this diet forms the dramatic climax of this first chapter.

A number of facts woven into this narrative set the tone for all that follows in the story of Daniel.

1. **The context: exile**
We are told that the unfolding story is taking place in the context of a forced removal from Jerusalem to Babylon. Though Daniel and his friends are well housed, well fed and well treated, they are effectively imprisoned. Far from home, they have lost the power and privilege associated with their prominent roles in Jewish life. Though it is separate from the Bible's main accounts of the exile, this is nonetheless an exile narrative, built

Day 2

on the dislocation and loss encountered on the journey from Jerusalem to Babylon.

2. The issue: faith

The taking of sacred articles from the temple in Jerusalem indicates that this is a spiritual as well as a political victory. There is a conflict between Babylon and Israel, in which Israel is the loser. But behind this there is an implied conflict between the gods of Babylon and Israel's God, Yahweh. One of the primary questions that the book of Daniel wrestles with is this: 'Is it Israel that has lost power, or *the God of Israel*?' On the surface, we wonder if Daniel can survive the experience of exile, but far more deeply the book is asking us if Yahweh can survive it. Is God's 'turf' limited to the Promised Land – or will he still be God when all appears lost?

3. The threat: assimilation

It is clear from the text that Nebuchadnezzar has initiated a programme of *assimilation* rather than *oppression*. His aim is to win Daniel and his friends over to the superiority and wisdom of the Babylonian worldview, and through them to influence other Jews. The decision to bring prominent members of a conquered culture into key roles in the service of the conquering empire is an established strategy of assimilation by which the empire gets the best out of each new territory it invades. Later in the book this benevolent assimilation will become harsh oppression, and the possibility of violence is never far below the surface, but in its wider context the narrative deals as much with *seduction* as with *suffering*.

4. the hero: Daniel

At the beginning of chapter 1, Daniel is one name amongst four: by the end of the chapter he is clearly the leader of the group. We aren't told whether this status was already in place in Jerusalem, but once in Babylon Daniel demonstrates the initiative, courage and faith that set him apart. The wisdom with which he *accepts* a new name but *rejects* the king's food marks him out as a leader of remarkable perception and creativity. We are presented, in the person of Daniel, with a model response to conditions of exile.

This chapter sets up the dramatic tension that is going to drive the unfolding of Daniel's story. What will become of the young man who has dared resist the emperor's will, question the power of the emperor's gods and subvert the superiority of the emperor's culture? Will the empire crush Daniel, or will he survive? Whose God will, in the long term, prove strongest?

Teaching Block 1:
Behind enemy lions: faith and exile in Daniel

1.1 What does the book of Daniel contain?
1.2 When was the book written?
1.3 When does the story take place?
1.4 What does Daniel have to teach us?
1.5 Does Daniel have value for today?

The time of the exile – the 70-year span in the sixth century when the Hebrew people lived as captives in Babylon – is a period of great significance in the history of Israel, particularly from a theological perspective. This traumatic time deeply changed the Hebrew view of God, and in many ways laid the foundations for the coming of the Messiah.

"It is difficult to overestimate the importance of the exile for the people of Israel. On the basis of what we now call the Sinai Covenant (set out in the Old Testament at, for example, Exodus 20–33), the special relationship between God and the people, with its promises and obligations on both sides, was set out. ... God's part of the deal involved making three

promises. First, Israel would have a land of its own. Second, the people of Israel would have descendants, so safeguarding the continuation of the nation for perpetuity. And third, God would always have a special relationship with them: they would be his people and he would be their God. ... This was the basis on which Israel as a nation was built. These were the marks of its distinctive identity of which it was so proud. Questions of meaning and purpose in life were explored against the background of these promises.

Imagine then what the exile represented..."
John Holdsworth[1]

In fact, the people of Israel should not have been surprised by the exile – there are plenty of hints in their earlier history that such a thing could happen and that their disobedience could trigger it. But for the most part they did not

read these signs, and it was the trauma of exile that finally convinced them that God was serious in both the promises and the sanctions of covenant. The prophets had spoken of it already, but it took the harsh reality of Babylon to bring the message home.

The book of Daniel is a particular window on this important time in Israel's life, personifying in its few main characters the Hebrew experience of exile. Just as the call of God's people was personified in Abraham and the worship of God's people in David, so the response of God's people to exile is personified in Daniel. If he can make it through, we all can. But while the events of this book are rooted in history, the narrative itself is not presented as a historical account. In order to grasp the way in which the theme of exile is treated in Daniel, it is important to encounter the text itself and to accept it on its own terms.

1.1 What does the book of Daniel contain?

The book of Daniel is set out in two distinct halves.

The first half – chapters 1 through 7 – outlines a series of stories of four young Jewish men exiled to the courts of Babylon in the sixth century BC.

The second half – chapters 8 through 12 – records a series of prophetic visions, attributed

to Daniel and dealing with a dramatic series of events that would lead up to the coming of God's kingdom.

The book was written partly in Hebrew (1:1 – 2:4[a] and 8–12) and partly in Aramaic (2:4[b] – 7:28). In the Jewish scriptures it appears among 'The Writings' while in our Bibles it is placed among The Prophets.

1.2 When was the book written?

Church tradition has generally viewed the book of Daniel as being written by Daniel in the sixth century, the period about which it speaks. A number of contemporary scholars have held to this view.

Modern critical scholarship has questioned this though, suggesting that the book was written in the second century: "When Jews were fighting for the survival of their faith against the brutal oppression of the Syrian ruler Antiochus Epiphanes. This was the time of Judas Maccabeus and the Maccabean revolt (167 BC)."
Stephen Travis[2]

Recent evangelical scholarship has suggested that the two views can be combined, in that parts of Daniel (essentially chapters 1–7) have their probable origin in a sixth century text whilst chapters 8–12 are a later, probably second century, composition to expound and comment on the earlier revelations of Daniel himself. The fact that surviving texts are partly Aramaic and partly Hebrew lends support to this possibility of a dual origin.

Day 2

1.3 When does the story take place?

Whatever dispute there might be about when exactly the book of Daniel was composed, there is no question as to when and where its action is set.

"The book of Daniel sets Daniel in the sixth century BC. There is no doubt or dispute about that. Major figures from this time period, known from other biblical and ancient Near Eastern sources, play an important role in the book: Nebuchadnezzar, Belshazzar, Cyrus, as well as Jehoiakim. Daniel 1:1 is dated to the third year of the reign of Jehoiakim (605 BC) and the latest references include one to the 'first year of King Cyrus' (1:21; 539 BC) as well as that great king's third year (10:1; 537 BC)."
Tremper Longman[3]

Daniel and his friends are part of the first group of exiles taken from Jerusalem to Babylon in 605 BC, 18 years before the full destruction of the city and its temple:

"This 605 BC expedition was the first of three major invasions of Palestine by Nebuchadnezzar son of Nabopolassar, the king of Babylon. The second occurred in 597 BC, when Jehoiachin, the son of Jehoiakim, was compelled by the Chaldeans to surrender Jerusalem (2 Kings 24:10–14) and go into captivity with all his princes and leaders, the flower of his army, and all the skilled craftsmen in his capital—including some of the priests, like young Ezekiel. The third and final captivity took place after the storming of Jerusalem in 587 BC, when all the people of Judah that had not escaped to the hills and joined the guerillas were taken into captivity in Babylonia."[4]

Daniel is recorded as having served in the Babylonian civil service, under a series of rulers, for around 70 years, until 536 BC, though the story continues beyond this 'retirement day' by several years. Since 536 BC was probably the year that the first of the Jews were allowed to return to Jerusalem under Zerubbabel (Ezra 2:2, Neh 7:7), Daniel's stay in Babylon overlaps fully with the Jewish experience of exile.

The later visions attributed to Daniel appear to cover the 400 years from the mid-sixth century to the mid-second century, though they also point beyond this date to the coming of God's greater kingdom. References to this are picked up in the New Testament particularly:

- By Jesus himself, especially in the use of the term 'Son of Man' – a term highlighted in the prophecies of Daniel (Matt 24:15, 24:30, 26:64; Mark 13:14, 13:26, 14:62; Luke 21:27, 22:69).

- By John in the book of Revelation (allusions throughout).

The underlying theme of these visions is the sovereignty of God in history. Despite appearances to the contrary, God remains in control. His plans are unchanged, and he will ultimately achieve, in history, that which he has set out to achieve. The apparent setback of the Babylonian captivity is a temporary condition, allowed by God to fulfil his greater plans. His will shall, in the end, still be done.

Issues of the origin, purpose, dating and authorship of the book of Daniel have vexed scholars for generations, certainly as much as any other biblical text. But as John Goldingay asserts, these issues, important as they are for an academic treatment of the book, have remarkably little impact on its meaning.

"Whether the stories are history or fiction, the visions actual prophecy or quasi-prophecy, written by Daniel or by someone else, in the sixth century BC or the second, or somewhere in between, makes surprisingly little difference to the book's exegesis. One understands the book on the basis of what it says..." John Goldingay[5]

1.4 What does Daniel have to teach us?

The book of Daniel is above all an account of 'faith in exile'. In the person of Daniel a drama is played out for the whole nation of Israel, as the Jews respond to the terrible loss of their land, city, throne and temple. Daniel's discovery that it is possible to maintain a robust faith in the face both of assimilation and of oppression is a message of hope for God's struggling people. Doubtless this is the function the book served in the second century BC, in the very difficult circumstances of Jerusalem under Antiochus Epiphanes, and it is the function it has served at other key points through the history both of Israel and of the church. In the journey from Jerusalem to Babylon there is a shattering of dreams, a loss of hope and confidence. But in the book of Daniel there is the re-discovery of an even greater dream – God's dream for a world made new.

"... the primary purpose for these texts is not to teach us how to behave, but rather to point us to God. Daniel is first and foremost a revelation of God. Now, God does not reveal himself to us in the abstract but rather in relationship to his people and through his actions in history. From the very first verses we see that this book is not essentially about Daniel, but rather about God. It is a revelation of who he is and how he acts for our redemption." Tremper Longman[6]

Like the books of the 'prophets of exile' – Jeremiah, Isaiah 40–55 and Ezekiel – the book of Daniel shows that a deeper, more robust faith emerges from the crucible of dislocation and loss. Exile, devastating as it was for those caught up in it, bore rich fruit for the Hebrew people, for the ongoing revelation of God's plans and for the theology of hope on which the coming of the Messiah was built.

"What we see is that the great trauma of the exile, potentially disastrous for the faith, identity and even existence of Israel, actually becomes one of the most creative periods in its theology with lots of new works being written and older traditions collected. It is because of this that we have an Old Testament at all." John Holdsworth[7]

1.5 Does Daniel have value for today?

The great tragedy of the book of Daniel is that controversies over its date and origins have rendered it 'off limits' to many readers. Its reputation as a difficult book, and its reliance on complex prophecies and dramatic dream-like images have frightened many Christians away from detailed study. We take the one or two stand-out stories and, usually out of context, build them into Sunday school lessons, but we don't dig deeper.

But Daniel has a great deal to teach us in the twenty-first century church, not least as an introduction to and exploration of the theme of exile. Believers living for God in difficult and complex situations can find strength and wisdom in these texts. In our own context, Daniel has much to offer Christians.

- Living or working in a pluralist or secular context. What does it mean to be a follower of Yahweh when all around you follow other gods?

- Passing through an 'exile' experience. Where is God when the things you thought were signs of his presence have been taken away from you?

- Longing to be a 'prophetic voice' for God's purposes. How do you communicate when the culture you live in has no knowledge of God's promises, and the church you belong to has forgotten them?

- Wrestling with the call to engage in political action and public life. How should God's people relate to governments and authorities that do not acknowledge his sovereign power?

- Seeking to live for God in their youth. Daniel demonstrates as a young man that it is possible to discern and follow God's will, even in the most difficult of circumstances.

Day 2

- Seeking to live for God in old age. The remarkable span of the book is such that we see Daniel *still* serving his God with courage and determination well into his retirement years.

- Looking for a spirituality for the real world. Is it possible, in the pains and pressures of urban life, to follow a devotional pattern that is deep, accessible, sustainable and sustaining?

- Suffering pressure and persecution, even to the point where their very lives are threatened. The dramatic stories of Daniel, Hananiah, Mishael and Azariah in the lions' den and in the furnace have given courage and strength for generations to the suffering church.

In The Zone

What might the book of Daniel have to offer the particular Zone you are exploring?

- *Faith and a Changing World*
  In what ways is Daniel relevant to the changing world of contemporary culture? What might 'daring to be a Daniel' mean in twenty-first century life?

- *Faith and the Developing World*
  How might the story of Daniel be seen in some of the different contexts faced by God's global family? Does 'daring to be a Daniel' have relevance in the developing world?

- *Faith and Devotional Life*
  How does the popular image of Daniel fuel and resource prayer? Is 'daring to be a Daniel' a devotional, or an activist, concept?

- *Faith and Everyday Life*
  The book of Daniel is set 2,600 years ago in Babylon. How can it speak to life in the UK today? What are the everyday contexts in which we might be challenged to 'dare to be a Daniel'?

- *Faith and Family Life*
  No mention is made of Daniel being married or having a family so can this book still address family issues? What does 'daring to be a Daniel' mean in the family and household?

- *Faith and Involvement*
  Daniel's consistency and courage are often quoted as a model for Christians in public life. Are there particular ways in which this book might speak to our contemporary context? What are the public implications of 'daring to be a Daniel' today?

- *Faith and Working Life*
  Daniel was a civil servant in a setting very different from our contemporary workplace. Can his experiences be of value to us today? What might 'daring to be a Daniel' look like in the world of work and career?

Question Time

The book of Daniel has vexed biblical scholars over many years, but has also provided the Christian faith with some of its most popular stories and images, and given us the phrase 'dare to be a Daniel'. Reflecting on the role this book has played in your life, ask yourself:

- What part has the character of Daniel played in my journey with God to date?

- What are the images and ideas that the phrase 'dare to be a Daniel' most readily brings to mind for you?

- Is the Daniel you have known someone you want to be like?

Teaching Block 2:
Learning from loss: faith and exile in Scripture

2.1 Exile as a tale of two cities

2.2 Exile as a second choice world

2.3 Exile as a tool of God's purposes

2.4 Exile as renewal and re-discovery

2.5 Exile as the normal Christian life

"Birds in flight, claims the architect Vincenzo Volentieri, are not between places, they carry their places with them. We never wonder where they live: they are at home in the sky, in flight. Flight is their way of being in the world." Geoff Dyer[8]

"We are pilgrims on earth, exiles journeying towards home. The world is passing away. We have God's word for it! Too much of our experience today militates against the fact that here in this life all symphonies remain unfinished." Ronald Rolheiser[9]

The heart of what it means to be in exile is to be away from home, cut off from the strength and structures in which we have been nurtured. Exile is a dislocation, a separation from that which has been familiar and on which we have depended. For the Hebrews taken from Jerusalem to Babylon, exile involved the loss of:

- The Promised Land – a potent symbol of God's victory and care

- The Temple – God's dwelling place on the earth

- The Holy City and Palace – symbols of God's reign established in his people

- The cycle of sacrifice, celebration and assembly – public opportunities to honour God's name.

In place of these comforting and familiar structures and symbols, the Hebrew exiles were plunged into a foreign world constructed in

Day 2

honour of foreign gods with a language, culture, history, customs, faith and society entirely alien to them.

A number of key aspects of the exile experience are evident through the narrative chapters of the book of Daniel.

Psalm 137:1-6 'Never forget you' (solo acoustic) (©Anon)
RL–Memories captured of the torment of the 'imprisonment' in Babylon ...

1–3 (verse)
The Babylon rivers flowed along,
But our tears nearly broke their banks;
Our hearts were wading in the rivers back home,
Our instruments dumb in this depression zone;
And what? They expected us to sing our songs?
These slave drivers request our party songs!

4–5 (bridge)
Just how? No way, impossible to do;
Sing of home when we're stuck in prison with you?
They're not just songs—they're our memories too;
And may my right hand forget how to strum if I ever forget you.

6 (chorus)
May my tongue get stuck to the top of my mouth if I ever forget you.
Jerusalem, I'll never forget you!
(Last two lines x 4)
The Street Bible[10]

2.1 Exile as a tale of two cities

Exile is symbolised in Scripture in the contrast between the two cities of Jerusalem and Babylon, symbolising the city we remember and long for and the city in which we must live.

"The city that Israel called 'The perfection of beauty, the joy of the whole world' is blockaded, assaulted, defeated, raped and pillaged by alien, pagan hands and feet." John Goldingay[11]

- **Jerusalem** – the city we long for is where God is publicly honoured. The structures of power flow towards the worship of our God. The courts make rulings in keeping with God's ways. The government passes laws that make obedience to God easy. The people we pass in the street share our faith and values, and encourage us along the way. The stories taught to our children are the stories we know and love. The flags that fly on public buildings honour the God we serve. Public festivals and celebrations give us opportunity to express our private faith. We are at home with our God and our God is at home with us.

- **Babylon** – the city in which we must live is where our faith becomes private. The structures of power conflict with the worship of our God. The courts make rulings that call into question God's ways. The government passes laws that make obedience to God costly. The people we pass in the street have beliefs and values very different from our own, and challenge our faith. The stories taught to our children are unfamiliar, perhaps frightening to us. The flags that fly on public buildings remind us that we are aliens here. Public festivals and celebrations bring tension, forcing us to choose between our own private faith and that expressed by our community. We are a long way from home and God, perhaps, seems a long way from us.

"Being propelled into exile is an experience of alienness, incomprehension, and abhorrence. In such circumstances, the commitment of faith might triumph, or at least survive, but it might wilt." John Goldingay[12]

Health Warning: It is important to note that

whilst 'Jerusalem' and 'Babylon' can symbolise these differences, the reality of life in these cities was never quite so black and white. In particular, the pre-exile prophets in Jerusalem often spoke of God's judgement on the city, because the apparent 'marriage' of state power and religious zeal was not grounded in true faith or obedience. Similarly it is easy for us to look back on a 'Christian' past through rose-tinted spectacles, while history itself may never have been quite as Christian as we think!

2.2 Exile as a second choice world

Viv Thomas provocatively describes this world of exile as a 'second choice' world. Our expectation, our hope, he writes, is that we will have the freedom to choose.

"Money, position and education are intended to give us the power to go for our preferred options and make our choices. In our ideal world we choose our job, spouse, city, entertainment, company, community and religion at leisure with freedom. Most of us like to have our first choice... ." Viv Thomas[13]

Daniel, by contrast, is a primary biblical example of 'second choice'.

"Daniel ... began his life as a young man with an appalling 'second choice'. When the Babylo-

nian army took Jerusalem Daniel was deported by the enemy. The Babylonians carted him off to Babylon. This was precisely the place where he did not want to be; he wanted to live in Jerusalem. The people he did not want to relate to were all the people who lived in Babylon. The culture of Babylon, its gods, food and language – all alien to him. The job eventually assigned to him was one he did not want – handling Babylon's administration. He had to respond continually to the dreams, whims, foolishness and political plotting of all the kings he served. ... Never in control of his own destiny, he was always someone's servant and had to be shaped constantly by the agenda of others. His life was one long adjustment to other people's thoughts, fears, passions and addictions." Viv Thomas[14]

2.3 Exile as a tool of God's purposes

Whilst the book of Daniel clearly presents the negative aspects of exile and the costs brought with it, it is very careful not to see exile, overall, as a negative experience. This is because of the assertion that lies at the heart of Daniel's story – that it is God himself who has handed his people over to Babylon in response to their sin, but with a view to repentance, not judgement.

"The responses affirmed within the Old Testament agree that the fall of Jerusalem is not to be explained by Yahweh's impotence or inactivity. Nor, as many people today might assume, was it merely the chance outworking

of political (and personality) factors. It is the deliberate act of Israel's own God." John Goldingay[15]

A central theme of the book of Daniel is the sovereignty of God. Time and again it is affirmed, even against the apparently limitless power of the Babylonian rulers, that it is God who is in control. Exile cannot ultimately destroy the faith of the Hebrews because it happens *within*, not *outside of*, the plans of their sovereign God.

"God's people were called to live in Babylon in a context dominated by superstition, omens

Day 2

and fear. Daniel and his Hebrew friends responded to this by embracing Babylon in every way possible, consistent with their responsibility to God. They chose to live their faith and yet be integrated into the heavily *contaminated world of Babylon. So, in the embrace of their second-choice world they affirmed that it was not Nebuchadnezzar, Belshazzar or Darius who was in control ... but God."* Viv Thomas[16]

2.4 Exile as renewal and re-discovery

"I can't be Japanese and I can't be Western – but I understand both. I am double-binded, but – and this is perhaps most important – I am also in a position that generates a great deal of energy and creativity." Arata Isozaki, describing his own brand of 'schizophrenic eclectic' architecture.[17]

Because exile does not negate the sovereignty of God, it becomes, for Daniel, a time of rich discovery, creativity and fruitfulness. For all the deprivations implied by the exile experience, Daniel is able to re-discover and explore the purposes of God at a deep and meaningful level. The extent to which the book of Daniel is referred to in the New Testament, and particularly Jesus' self-identification as the 'Son of Man' (prophesied in Daniel 7:13 and 8:17) confirm the extent to which Daniel has come, through the experience of exile, to a deeper understanding of the purposes of God in history.

"Daniel lived in a huge imaginative world where God spoke in images, visions and dreams. The rationalism and activism which is the mark of so much evangelicalism today did not trap Daniel; he lived with the immediacy of the celestial world and in rich encounter with God." Viv Thomas[18]

The exile is a turning point in the history of Israel – arguably the point from which the

promise of the Messiah becomes most real. In the life and history of Daniel and his friends, it is a cruel interruption to progress: but in the wider purposes of God it is a watershed period, carrying forward God's salvation purposes. The Bible presents the fall of Jerusalem in 587 BC as a pivotal point in the theological history of Israel, a period from which emerges "some of the boldest and most eloquent theological probing in the Old Testament".[19] In the crisis of life and faith that the exile represents, Walter Brueggemann suggests, God's people had two tasks.

"To let go of the old world of king and temple that God had now taken from [them]", and *"To receive from God's hand a new world."* Walter Brueggemann[20]

This resonates, he suggests, with the whole witness of Scripture, in which 'learning through loss' is an abiding theme. Exile, in this view, is not a sign of God's defeat so much as a sign of his creativity. It is his mysterious way of bringing to birth a new hope for Israel – a hope that does not long simply for the recent past of temple and palace, but looks further back to the very origins of the promises of God and further forward to God's promised future.

Because of the character and faithfulness of God, exile turns *nostalgia* into *hope*.

2.5 Exile as the normal Christian life

"The man who finds his homeland sweet is still a tender beginner; he to whom every soil is as his native one is already strong: but he is perfect to whom the entire world is as a foreign land." Hugo of St Victor[21]

In the New Testament, the experience of exile becomes normative for the Christian community. Filled with the power of the risen Christ, the

church is sent *into exile* in the world, to bring the presence of God to every people, tribe, place and culture:

- When the disciples ask Jesus in Acts 1 *"are you at this time going to restore the kingdom to Israel?"* they are assuming that Christ's triumph will bring the end of exile. Jerusalem will be restored as the epicentre of God's global plan and the people of every tribe and nation will be drawn to God's visible, public, structured and established new order. Jesus insists this remains a future promise, and in the meantime, his people are called to *"be my witnesses in Jerusalem, and in all Judea and Samaria, and to the ends of the earth."* They are to carry the gospel into every culture – known and unknown, familiar and foreign. The call of the gospel is a call *into* exile.

- This leads to the important New Testament concept of Christians as 'aliens and strangers' (Heb 11:13 1 Pet 1:1, 2:11) living freely in the world and yet not at home within it. The Greek terms *paroikeo* and *paroiko* present the local church as a colony of resident aliens in a given place and time. We are called to be both *resident* and *alien*, at home but not at home, in every place to which the Spirit of God scatters us.

"1 Peter begins by identifying the readers with those in exile ... As Daniel and his colleagues in Babylon had to learn how to sing the Lord's song in a foreign land, so too the Christians in Pontus, Galatia, Cappadocia, Asia and Bithynia are being encouraged to sing a new song, a song about Jesus and his saving grace, in the place where they too are scattered aliens." Peter Phillips[22]

Ernest Lucas suggests three aspects of Daniel's life in exile that point to ways in which Christian colonies of resident aliens should view their culture:

1. Daniel's refusal to adopt a ghetto mentality in exile. He was ready to engage with this alien culture, even taking the opportunity to spend three years studying it in order to understand it in some depth. He accepted a responsible job in its power structure.

2. Within this context, Daniel was concerned to retain his personal integrity. Engaging fully with the alien culture did not mean being absorbed in it with the loss of his distinctiveness, especially his commitment to God. At this point his stand is made privately: only a couple of Babylonian officials know of it.

3. Daniel adopted a non-confrontational, conciliatory attitude in his relations with the Babylonian officials. He did not make life unnecessarily hard for them, nor did he demand they behave in a way that would risk their jobs or lives. He found a creative way to achieve his end.[23]

Question Time

A significant question that is implied throughout the book of Daniel is this, What is *lost* and what is *gained* on the journey from Jerusalem to Babylon? We know there are many things we lose in the experience of exile, but are there also things we gain? Taking this question as a starting point, ask yourself this.

- For Daniel and his friends, what advantages did they have in Jerusalem that were no longer available in Babylon?

- By contrast, what advantages or opportunities did they discover in Babylon that they might never have found had they stayed put?

- What difference might this make to my perception of the changes in my own culture and context?

Day 2

In The Zone

How might a theology of exile impact your approach to the Zone you are exploring?

- *Faith and a Changing World*
  What examples are there in today's culture of a 'loss' or 'second choice' situation that might turn out to have hidden advantages and fruitfulness? Is Daniel's journey into Babylon a good model for twenty-first century discipleship?

- *Faith and the Developing World*
  What contemporary experiences of exile are shaping the global family of God? How might seeing exile as the normal Christian life encourage Christians in the developing world?

- *Faith and Devotional Life*
  What is the place of lament in Christian devotional spirituality? How might a theology of exile inform and shape our prayers? Does an understanding of second choice worlds help us to pray for ourselves and for others?

- *Faith and Everyday Life*
  How has learning from loss featured in your journey with God so far? Are there second choice areas in your life? How might a theology of exile shape your response?

- *Faith and Family Life*
  In what ways might learning from loss be important in family life? Is a theology of exile helpful at these times? What are the second choice worlds presented to us as families?

- *Faith and Involvement*
  How does a theology of exile affect the Christian view of power? Are there specific issues in British public life today in which, for Christians, questions of power and exile will be raised?

- *Faith and Working Life*
  How does the idea of a second choice world relate to those dissatisfied with their job or career, or facing difficulties in the workplace? Does an understanding of exile offer new ways of dealing with these situations?

Voices From Exile:
Yioula Taliadorou

(Yioula Taliadorou works with Christian development agency Tearfund in London. She experienced exile in 1974, as a teenager, when her family were forced by political changes to leave their home on the beautiful island of Cyprus.)

My worst nightmare as a child was the possibility of losing my home. Growing up in a very beautiful country in the midst of a warm, loving community, I didn't want my world to change. All the people I loved and everything that mattered to me was connected to that place. I learned about community there. I knew I was unconditionally loved and could move around without fear. We shared common roots and family stories going back for generations were often recounted. I knew I belonged and that felt very comfortable.

All I have now are the memories of a world and a life I once knew. The dramatic events of the summer of 1974 changed the world as I knew it for good. A young teenager by then, I had to face a journey that was difficult both emotionally and physically as we made our way to London. Seeing my home fall apart and the pain that brought to the people I cared about was often too hard to bear. The experience can only be described as a prolonged bereavement that refuses to go away. But as always, God found a way of helping and transforming me. The tasks of adapting to a new home, learning a new language and completing my education kept me busy. During those times I really learned to trust God. My new environment changed from an overwhelming unknown to a series of new challenges and discoveries.

I still miss the endless sunshine, the warm blue sea, the smiling people, the open houses with limitless hospitality and the luscious fruits. In return, I have discovered a city that never sleeps, the world on my doorstep and a new depth in my relationship with God. When you have all your material possessions taken away and all the things you put your trust in vanish, then God takes centre stage in your life. During the difficult times I found God to be very close, helping me to realise that 'all things work together for good...' (Rom 8:28). It is one thing to have head-knowledge of this verse; it is another thing to experience it right at the core of your being. I knew then that God not only *could* but *would* bring something good out of the mess that brought so much pain. His compassion was and is very precious to me, something I want to share with hurting people.

Deep down I don't want anyone else to go through what I went through. Sadly my story is not unique. Millions of people today, both young and old, experience exile. My work with Tearfund has become, for me, an effective channel to reach out with compassion to these broken human beings.

Day 2

Teaching Block 3:
Minority report: faith and exile today

3.1 What is (or was) Christendom?
3.2 What is (or will be) post-Christendom?
3.3 Is this exile?
3.4 How should the church respond?
3.5 What are the transitions we will face?

"Imagine you have travelled to a country where few people are Christians; where biblical values do not pervade society; where most people do not even know the basic outline of the Bible story. Welcome home. This is Britain today." Tim Chester and Steve Timmis[24]

"It took several centuries to convert Britain to Christianity, but it has taken less than forty years to forsake it." Callum Brown[25]

Exile: Are we there yet?

The religious landscape of Europe changed almost beyond recognition through the second half of the 20th century. Social commentators have summed up this change by describing a shift from a 'Christendom' to a 'post-Christendom' society. Where the Christian faith once dominated European society, dictating its beliefs and assumptions, influencing its politics and laws, shaping its art and architecture and holding the hearts of its people – it is now for most a distant memory, a fast-fading echo from a past we are leaving behind.

"Western civilisation is still defined by Christianity, but as a civilisation that used to be Christian." Robert Jensen[26]

For a number of theologians and missiologists, this decline of the Christian church in Britain and across Europe is viewed as a kind of journey into exile. The Christendom period, during which Christianity was the dominant faith and its churches held wealth, power and prestige, is seen as a parallel of the pre-exilic Jerusalem, when temple and palace worked together and faith was enshrined as a national possession. The exile period, when so much of this was lost and the Hebrew deportees were forced to work out their faith in an alien culture, is likened to our current post-Christendom status, when we *remember* the social dominance of the Christian faith of yesterday, but don't *experience* it today.

"You may not have noticed or cared, since it has had so little effect recently, but that dubiously vain rooster called Christendom – the organisational inbreeding of religion, culture and state – has gone the way of all flesh. ... Make no mistake: the cultural phenomenon of Christendom is dead." James Berkley[27]

If this is the case, and the parallels between Israel's journey from Jerusalem to Babylon and ours from a Christendom to a post-Christendom context are seen to stand, then we have much to learn from those who, thousands of years ago, confronted the reality of exile and survived.

"We too face a point at which God appears to be terminating our known world and inviting us to a new world in which the true nature of the church and its mission can be recovered." David Smith[28]

Health Warning: Whilst the changes in the place of Christianity in our culture are real and measurable, and the parallel with an 'exile' experience is valid, it is very important not to over-state the stages of this transition. In particular we should note:

• Christianity, though weakened, is by no means absent from our culture. Like the smile of the Cheshire Cat in *Alice in Wonderland*, which remained visible long after the cat had disappeared, there are aspects of Christendom that are still very much present in our everyday lives.

- Recent trends, no matter how clearly visible, do not *necessarily* tell us what the future holds. A number of commentators have noted in the early years of the millennium that the 'radical secularisation' of the late 20th century has not continued in quite the ways expected, and that after the collapse of European communism it is *atheism* that seems tired and outdated in our age.

These observations should not stop us from learning the lessons of the Hebrew exile as a parable of our times, but they may save us from over-stating the case.

3.1 What is (or was) Christendom?

"Christendom is the name given to the sacral culture that has dominated European society from around the eleventh century until the end of the twentieth. Its sources go back to the time when Constantine came to the throne of the Roman Empire and granted Christians complete freedom of worship, and even favoured Christianity, thereby undermining all other religions in the empire." Michael Frost and Alan Hirsch[29]

In its loosest sense, Christendom is a term used to describe the Christian world: those areas of the world in which Christianity has become the dominant faith. More particularly, though, Christendom describes the coming together of spiritual and temporal power when the Christian faith becomes so established in a culture that matters of faith (church government, theology, moral guidance, Christian education, public worship) come to overlap to a significant degree with matters of public life (state government, political theory, law and order, education, social events). In Europe, the Christendom period is broadly seen to cover the eleventh to the twentieth centuries.

"Church spires dominated the landscape; church bells pealed out across the countryside; church ceremonies punctuated the rhythm of the seasons and major life events. Churches 'hatched, matched and dispatched' everyone in their parish. Bishops and abbots were not only spiritual leaders but involved in economic management and political activities." Stuart Murray[30]

The roots of Christendom, when spiritual and temporal power first came together, are generally seen in the conversion in AD 312 of Emperor Constantine (274–337). Formerly a worshipper of the sun god Sol, Constantine was the first emperor to embrace Christianity and in 313 he issued the Edict of Milan, granting freedom of worship to Christians throughout the empire. The remainder of his reign was marked by the giving of significant social favours and financial support to Christians, confirming that Christianity had moved from the margins of Roman society to its very heart. This single event led to a long period in which the church became the dominant force in European politics, society and culture: a situation that the philosophical and social changes of more recent centuries have worked to undermine.

Christian historians are by no means in agreement as to the gains and losses of the Christendom era. Some accept the development of state churches as the inevitable result of Christianity's growth. Others see the marriage of church and state as the source of all manner of social and theological ills. Most find themselves somewhere in between, seeing both the blessing and the curse in the Christendom context. There is broad agreement, though, on the key features that make up the idea of Christendom.

- There is a 'marriage' between spiritual and temporal authority, creating frequent overlaps between church and state, faith and politics, discipleship and social life.

- Nations, as well as individuals and groups, come to be described as 'Christian'.

- Birth and nationality, rather than conversion and personal faith, become the arbiters of Christian identity.

- Christian believers, whether nominal or committed, hold majority status and benefit from the resultant political influence and social privilege.

Day 2

- The voice of the church is given privileged status in public discourse, pushing other voices to the margins.

- The wider culture, especially in terms of art and architecture, is deeply influenced by questions of Christian faith and theology.

Whatever assessment is given to the strengths and weaknesses of Christendom, three things are agreed by commentators across the spectrum.

- This is a reality by which European culture has been most deeply shaped through its formative centuries.

- This is a reality by which many of our current assumptions about faith and church have also been shaped.

- This is a reality that is now changing or has changed, calling us to re-visit our understanding of the church's role and mission in a new cultural context.

"All the major church traditions in this country have been shaped by Christendom – by an expectation that they have a special right to be heard and that people 'ought' to listen to them. Whole strategies of evangelism have been based on residual guilt about not going to church. But we are now one voice among many." Graham Cray[31]

3.2 What is (or will be) post-Christendom?

"Britain is showing the world how religion as we have known it can die." Callum Brown[32]

The term 'post-Christendom' has emerged in recent years as a way of describing our new context, in which the end of Christianity's privileged status is a major factor.

"The church has indeed lost its role as the keystone in the arch of European culture." Grace Davie[33]

Factors in this change include:

- The massive decline in the second half of the twentieth century in church attendance; a decline seen to varying degrees throughout Western culture and across the denominational spectrum.
  → If the current rate of decline is not arrested, the Methodist Church will have zero membership by 2037.
  → If it continues to shrink at the present rate, the Church of Scotland will close its last congregation in 2033.
  → Unless something happens to reverse the decline it is experiencing, the Anglican Church in Wales will be unsustainable by 2020.
  → The Salvation Army and United Reformed Church face similar prospects.
  → Attendance at mass in Roman Catholic

churches fell from nearly two million to just over one million between 1965 and 1996.
  → Almost all the indicators in the period 1980–2000 show accelerating decline in the Church of England, with Sunday attendance figures below one million for the first time.[34]

- The resultant shift in the patterns of wider social behaviour previously associated with church membership.

"In unprecedented numbers, the British people since the 1960s have stopped going to church, have allowed their church membership to lapse, have stopped marrying in church and have neglected to baptise their children. Meanwhile, their children, the two generations who grew to maturity in the last thirty years of the twentieth century, stopped going to Sunday School, stopped entering confirmation or communicant classes, and rarely, if ever, stepped inside a church to worship in their entire lives." Callum Brown[35]

- The growing crisis for Christian churches as they attempt to adapt to this new context.

"For the last forty years, the statistics have reflected an accelerated crisis in church life, and we are now faced with the serious

possibility – likelihood, even – that the Christian faith might disappear entirely from our culture within the first half of this century. ... Our churches are in incredibly bad shape. Moreover, the decline is affecting all Christian traditions. Every denomination faces the same issues, and they extend right across the theological spectrum." John and Olive Drane[36]

3.3 Is this exile?

"As Christians enter the twenty-first century, they do so as exiles, strangers and pilgrims, aliens in a strange land. They will need to learn the strategies of survival, and to sing the songs of Zion in the midst of Babylon." Kenneth Leech[37]

Both the scale and the nature of these changes have led a number of theologians to see the current context of the church as a kind of exile, drawing parallels between our present journey and that of the Hebrews from Jerusalem to Babylon. Particular parallels are seen in:

- The loss of the symbols of political power, public acceptance and social prestige for believers who are plunged into an alien and sometimes hostile environment.

- The need to communicate faith in a 'market-place' of competing truth claims.

- The pervading sense that vibrant faith is a feature of the past, but not of the future.

- The need to deal with the apparent failure of Christianity to hold the hearts of the majority.

- The creeping fear that behind this failure of the church we might be witnessing, in fact, the failure of God himself.

"From the viewpoint of a human observer, it seemed that the religion of the Hebrews had been completely discredited. Their God, Yahweh, had apparently shown himself inferior in power to the mighty gods of Assyria and Babylon ... When they levelled Yahweh's temple to the ground and burned its ruins, the Babylonian troops served notice to all the world that their gods were mightier than Yahweh, no matter what titles the Hebrews gave him."[38]

3.4 How should the church respond?

"It is in the nature of mission always to seek the frontier where the struggle between faith and unfaith is most clearly and urgently drawn. The first essential of leadership, the one above all others with regard to mission, is to see the vision of the reign of God being established in these frontier situations and then to hold that before the church. All else is secondary." Wilbert Shenk[39]

Just as the experience of exile ultimately became one of renewal for the Hebrew people, so there are a number of positive ways in which we might, as twenty-first century disciples, respond to these changes.

- **Mission: new learning opportunities.**
  Post-Christendom culture presents us with

significant challenges – but might these challenges also offer us opportunities to re-discover the mission of God in our culture, and to learn again what it might mean to be a vital force for mission in society? One impact of such questioning is that we have the opportunity to 'become a beginner' – to think about church, worship, discipleship, fellowship and the life of faith *as if we were doing it all for the first time.*

- **Flexibility: new opportunities for change.**
  In a Christendom culture the church is a fixed building at the very centre of culture and society. Heavily structured, unmoving and unchanging, it is the anchor at the heart of all else, as was the Temple and Holy City for the Jews. In exile, this changes. Our faith

becomes mobile, transferable, adaptable and creative, responding to the range of different circumstances in which we find ourselves. Pete Ward has suggested that this calls for a 'liquid church' – a church whose structures and systems are fluid enough to take different shapes in different places. This will be a church built on networks of relationships through which Christ is communicated.[40]

- **Access: new opportunities to make contact.** A church in exile can offer access to faith for people whose own experience is of exile. According to sociologist Robert Wuthnow, mobility and exile are the everyday experience of increasing numbers of people in Western culture. This leads to a shift from a spirituality of 'dwelling' to a spirituality of 'seeking', and invites us to reach out to people whose experience is more of homelessness than of home.[41]

"At one time people were residents of their communities; now they are commuters. Thus images of stable dwellings have increasingly been replaced by images of those who have left home: the migrant worker, the exile, the refugee, the drifter, the person who feels alienated or displaced, the person lost in the cosmos, the travelling salesman, the lonesome net surfer, the lonely face in the crowd, the marginal person, the vagrant, the dispossessed or homeless person." Robert Wuthnow[42]

3.5 What are the transitions we will face?

Stuart Murray is convinced that the shift from a Christendom to post-Christendom setting is highly significant for the church, and has summarised the implications in terms of seven key transitions. This 'journey into exile', he says, will take the church:

- **From the centre to the margins:** In Christendom the Christian story and the churches were central, but in post-Christendom, they are marginal.

- **From majority to minority:** In Christendom Christians comprised the (often overwhelming) majority, but in post-Christendom we are a minority.

- **From settlers to sojourners:** In Christendom Christians felt at home in a culture shaped by their story, but in post-Christendom we are aliens, exiles and pilgrims in a culture in which we no longer feel at home.

- **From privilege to plurality:** In Christendom Christians enjoyed many privileges, but in post-Christendom we are one community among many in a plural society.

- **From control to witness:** In Christendom churches could exert control over society, but in post-Christendom we exercise influence only through our witnessing to our story and its implications.

- **From maintenance to mission:** In Christendom the emphasis was on maintaining a supposedly Christian status quo, but in post-Christendom it is on mission within a contested environment.

- **From institution to movement:** In Christendom churches operated mainly in institutional mode, but in post-Christendom we must become again a Christian movement.[43]

In The Zone

What might these seven transitions mean in terms of the specific Zone you are exploring?

- *Faith and a Changing World*
  What are the signs in the wider culture that these changes are happening, and that they will re-shape the church? What new models of church are emerging to face these challenges?

- *Faith and the Developing World*
  How different is the situation faced by the Christian church outside the sphere of Western culture? What lessons can the Western church learn from the places where the global family of God is in a pre-Christendom or non-Christendom context, and where the Christian church has always been a marginal, minority community?

- *Faith and Devotional Life*
  What kinds of prayer will this new context call for? How might these transitions change the nature and practice of the Christian devotional life? What kinds of images and metaphors – and what sections of Scripture – will most feed us through this time of change?

- *Faith and Everyday Life*
  How is the shape of church likely to change in response to these transitions? What can you do as an individual to prepare for these changes and contribute constructively to them?

- *Faith and Family Life*
  What are the implications of these changes for the ways in which we educate and nurture our children in the Christian faith? What new circumstances might we need to prepare them for?

- *Faith and Involvement*
  How do these transitions change the role of a believer serving in politics and public life? What specific challenges might these transitions present to a Christian serving in local government, as a school governor or as a charity trustee?

- *Faith and Working Life*
  How do these transitions affect the way the Christian faith is perceived in the workplace? What kind of attitudes and practices should post-Christendom Christians adopt?

Question Time

Take a look at the seven transitions cited above and ask yourself:

- Where is my local church in terms of each of these seven? Is this a transition we have made, are making or have yet to make?

- Where does the denomination or network I belong to stand? What are the signs that these transitions are already shaping our strategies and expectations?

- What about my own attitudes, practices and expectations? Do these transitions help to explain some of the struggles I have faced? How might my understanding of faith, discipleship, church and mission be changed by these transitions?

Day 2

Conclusion:
I am with you always

The power of God's people to live in exile derives, above all, from God's presence with them. In a comment on Ephesians 3:17, in which Paul writes "I pray that Christ will make his home in your hearts through faith" (Good News Bible), John Stott points out that the basis on which God dwells with us is contrasted to our own exiled condition:

"There are two similar Greek verbs, paroikeo and katoikeo. The former is the weaker. It means to inhabit (a place) as a stranger, to live in fact as a paroikos, the very word Paul has used in Ephesians 2:19 for an alien who is living away from his home. Katoikeo, on the other hand, means to settle down somewhere. It refers to a permanent as opposed to a temporary abode, and is used metaphorically both for the fullness of the Godhead abiding in Christ and for Christ's abiding in the believer's heart. ... Paul prays to the Father that Christ by his Spirit will be allowed to settle down in their hearts, and from his throne there both control and strengthen them." John Stott[44]

Our calling as followers of Jesus may be to live in exile while we await the coming of God's kingdom – to be resident aliens scattered through his world. But there is no such ambiguity in God's promise to dwell within us. Christ dwells in our hearts by his Spirit *permanently* and *unambiguously*: He is not a resident alien in our lives; he has made our hearts his home.

Daniel's discovery in Babylon, where he was torn away from Jerusalem and the Temple and yet found that God was with him in his exile, could be summarised as: "You can take me away from God's presence, but you can't take God's presence away from me."

In Christ, this becomes the permanent, guaranteed condition of the saints. We can live by faith through any exile, because nothing can disrupt Christ's presence in us.

Voices in Exile:
The Subterranean Shoe Room

The Subterranean Shoe Room is a very cool retro-show store in the hippest part of perpetually cool San Francisco. It was opened on Valencia Street this year by an unlikely proprietor. Brock Bingaman is a Southern Baptist church planter and evangelist who came to San Francisco with every intention of planting a conventional purpose-driven type church. He had planted churches before and one conversation with him reveals that he is an evangelist to the core. But San Francisco is crawling with failed conventional purpose-driven type church planters. So secular, so culturally vigorous, so pro-gay is the city that the conventional churches are withering on the vine. Crestfallen, young Brock realized that there was no point trying to re-create what many had tried and failed at before him. Needing gainful employment, Brock says he turned to his first love – shoes!

You see, Brock is the Imelda Marcos of the Southern Baptist Convention. Ever since he was a boy, he has collected shoes. He loves the darn things. When we told him we only own two or three pairs each, he scoffed. 'I buy two or three pairs a week!' he laughed. Together with his brother Josh and their wives, he rented a shop and filled it with new and retro (restored second-hand) shoes. Now he's doing a roaring trade in a fashion district that until the Subterranean Shoe Room opened only had a sports shoe outlet.

Brock has a special gift when it comes to shoes, though. He's no ordinary shoe salesman. He strikes up a conversation with those who browse his collection, and when they tell him they're not sure what they're looking for, he has a standard retort: 'Tell me about yourself and I'll tell you the shoes you need.' And so scores of San Franciscans have opened their lives to him. After hearing their story, Brock tells them he has just the thing they're looking for and pulls out a pair of pink Pumas or cherry-red Docs. And he seems to get it right every time.

"As a church planter, I spent ninety per cent of my time with Christians," he moans. "Now, as a shoe salesman, I spend ninety per cent of my time with non-Christians." He has developed significant relationships with gay couples, Marxist professors, ageing hippies and bohemian artists. Just the kind of people you don't find in church. ... It's a tough town to evangelise, and Brock has struck on a natural way to incarnate the message of the gospel to a people group normally hostile to Christianity.[45]

Voices in Exile:
Listening to those outside the faith

If we want to reach our nation, we must first listen to it.

In November 2002, the London Institute for Contemporary Christianity conducted a research exercise with the aim of capturing the voice of post-Christendom Britain. Researcher Nick Spencer conducted interviews with forty individuals who identified themselves as agnostic – ie who expressed neither a definite belief in, nor a definite rejection of, the existence of God. According to the 1998 Social Trends Survey of the Office for National Statistics, this definition covers some 66 per cent of the current UK population. These forty respondents were given free reign to express their views on religion, faith and church in Britain today. The research was professionally monitored and ratified, and its broad aim was to explore three main topics.

* Individual attitudes to Christianity
* Personal beliefs
* The perceived barriers to Christian faith today.

The results of this research were collated in a report, *Beyond Belief? Barriers and Bridges to Faith Today* (London Institute for Contemporary Christianity, 2003). The report carries direct quotations from the respondents and an analysis of their views in the light of wider academic research into religion in Britain today. Data is presented in terms of barriers to faith that are cultural, personal, ecclesiastical and intellectual. In response, the report offers suggestions as to how bridges can be built to Britain's unbelieving majority, in terms of these same four categories.

The overall result is a captivating – and sobering – insight into the reasons people give for not engaging with the church, making the report essential reading for all those seeking to re-imagine the role of the church in a changing culture. How significant might it be for us to listen more closely and attentively to the voices of those who are in exile from the church itself?

"It's a paradox in a way, isn't it? ... People that are Christians, aren't."

"Most of the trouble around the world is caused by religion."

"The spiritual person doesn't really look at things in terms of right and wrong."

"It was nice to believe that Santa exists, too."

"The inflexibility of them. You know, even when you go and seek them out, and even if you only want a part of their lifestyle or a part of their beliefs they are not willing. They want you to have the whole package. And not all of us need that in our lives."

"There is no evidence to support anything in the Bible."

"Christianity sometimes kind of cloaks itself. ... They like to think of themselves as being kind of Christian, but I think in my understanding of the word they are not."

"I don't believe in a God, I believe that when you die your spirit lives on and that, you know, the spirit watches over you. Not God, not Jesus, nobody else, just, you know, somewhere up there in the ether, an atom is floating about looking after me."

"My head tells me there isn't a God, but my heart wants to believe it."

"Is that a part of the Bible then, War and Peace?"

Day 2

Voices in Exile:
Books to read in Babylon

A provocative and valuable resource is Stuart Murray's major work *Post-Christendom: Church and Mission in a Strange New World* (Paternoster, 2004). Writing from the perspective of the Anabaptist movement, Murray is highly critical of the Christendom marriage of church and state, and sees the transition into a post-Christendom culture as an opportunity to rediscover a richer, more biblical faith. His chapter on 'Post-Christendom Resources' suggests a whole range of ways in which the Christian community might engage with post-Christendom culture: this chapter alone is worth the cover price of the book! Recommended for all those wanting to think more deeply about the challenge of the shift from a Christendom to a post-Christendom society.

Viv Thomas's *Second Choice: Embracing life as it is* (Paternoster, 2000). A creative and inspiring study of the life of Daniel. Forced to live in the second choice world of exile, Daniel is a model for all those whose lives are not as perfectly situated as they might have hoped – those who face limitations, pressures, trials and inconveniences of every kind. To live our lives well, Viv Thomas asserts, it is vital that we learn how to survive and thrive in worlds of second choice – or of no choice at all. Recommended for all those who have ever wondered why God allows periods of 'exile' in our lives.

The Shaping of Things to Come: Innovation and Mission for the 21st Century Church (Hendrickson, 2003) is a significant and valuable resource from Australians Alan Hirsch and Mike Frost. Looking at models not only in Australia but also in Europe and North America, Hirsch and Frost encourage us to rediscover what it will mean to be a 'missional' church, interacting creatively and confidently with our post-Christendom culture. Full of examples, quotes and practical suggestions, this book will challenge and inspire a new generation of missionaries to recapture the 'lost' cultures of the post-Christendom West.

Pete Ward's *Liquid Church* (Paternoster, 2002) is an attempt to imagine 'a different way of being church'. Calling for a shift towards adaptable, flexible structures defined by relationships more than by boundaries, *Liquid Church* is a provocative and insightful book, written essentially from an Anglican perspective, and highly relevant to the church in the current UK context. Recommended for leaders, students and all those seeking to re-imagine church for a new context.

The transatlantic partnership of Martin Robinson and Dwight Smith brings theory and practice together in *Invading Secular Space: Strategies for Tomorrow's Church* (Monarch, 2003). Their starting point is the sorry state of the church in much of Western culture: but decline need not, they say, lead to despair. Exploring issues of church, mission and leadership, Robinson and Smith believe that the Christian community can once again become a movement for change in the post-Christendom West. Recommended for leaders, students and all those planning or engaging in mission through the local church.

Red Moon Rising (Survivor, 2003) by Pete Greig and Dave Roberts is the story of 24-7 Prayer: a movement of prayer and mission that began by accident in 1999 and is now active in more than fifty countries. One of the genuinely 'good news' stories of the church's recent history, *Red Moon Rising* will inspire you, challenge you and quite possibly provoke you to action. Find out why it is that thousands of young adults across the globe are discovering a fresh, passionate and life-changing commitment to prayer that is 'at home' in a postmodern, post-Christendom world. Recommended for anyone with a pulse, a prayer life and a passion for today's generation.

Europe: The Exceptional Case: Parameters of Faith in the Modern World (*Darton Longman & Todd, 2002*) by Grace Davie is a unique and insightful exploration of church attendance in Europe by comparison to four other key global areas. Academic but accessible, Davie's argument challenges many of our assumptions about the 'secularisation' of our culture, and creates strong grounds for hope for the emergence of new patterns of Christian affiliation in Europe's new context. Recommended for leaders, students and all those engaged in mission in contemporary culture.

David Smith's ***Mission After Christendom*** (*Darton Longman & Todd, 2002*) is an academic study of the prospects for Christian mission in our changing context. Written with intelligence, passion and broad cultural awareness, *Mission After Christendom* challenges many of our assumptions about the nature of Christian mission, and particularly about Europe as the 'sending' continent. Recommended for leaders, students and all those engaging in mission in contemporary culture.

Prophecy:
Faith for the future

Outline of the Day:

Introduction: Prophecy

Overview: Daniel 2 and 7

Introduction: Prophecy

"With Zion a smoking ruin and a bewildered and lamenting remnant living as strangers in a land with a brilliant and powerful culture which owed nothing to their faith in Yahweh, the urgent and desperate need was for a new word of comfort and renewed vision and hope." David Smith[46]

"The prophets worked to get people who were beaten down to open themselves up to hope in God's future. In the wreckage of exile and death and humiliation and sin, the prophet ignited hope, opening lives to the new work of salvation that God is about at all times and everywhere." Eugene Peterson[47]

Chapters 2 and 7 of the book of Daniel both deal with prophetic dreams. After the scene-setting introduction afforded by chapter 1, chapter 2 plunges immediately into the heart of the action with Daniel's God-given capacity to interpret dreams being used to impact the highest level of Babylonian society – the king himself. We are introduced to a central theme of the book: the God in heaven who is able to reveal mysteries. Daniel is cast in the role of a prophet who stands between God and the pagan king. The prophet's own dream, recorded in chapter 7, takes this theme further, and forms a bridge into the apocalyptic visions of chapters 8 to 12, in which the curtain is raised on the future destiny of nations.

'Apocalyptic' is a particular genre of biblical material, offering God-given insight into the big picture of global history and destiny. Ernest Lucas suggests two key ways in which the term apocalyptic can be applied:

"Firstly, it is used of a form of literature, one characteristic of which is its use of visions with symbolic imagery, which is sometimes quite bizarre (e.g. Daniel 7 and 8; Revelation).

"Secondly, it is a particular form of eschatology which highlights God's control of history and the struggle between good and evil coming to a climax at 'the time of the end' with the final intervention of God to establish his kingdom."[48]

Along the way, we see Daniel exercising a prophetic ministry in three key areas:

- **As an individual** as Daniel's remarkable gift for knowing and interpreting dreams is used by God to influence successive kings; to save the lives of Daniel and his friends; to secure a safe future for the exiles and to establish through the narrative the ultimate authority of Yahweh, even in Babylon.

- **In society** as he delivers God's word of accountability and judgement to the Babylonian kings, resulting in examples both of repentance and of judgement.

- **In the big picture** as glimpses are given of God's future plans, not only for the immediate context of the book, but for the kingdom that is to be revealed and the coming of the one who will appear 'as a Son of Man'.

> **Key verse:**
> No wise man, enchanter, magician or diviner can explain to the king the mystery he has asked about, but there is a God in heaven who reveals mysteries …
> Daniel 2:27

The prophetic elements of Daniel have been a significant source of controversy over many years, and have all but derailed the interpretation of the book for some commentators: but they persist as a vital, central aspect of the narrative. The assertion that 'there is a God in heaven who reveals mysteries' (2:28) is an interpretive key to the book. Whether this is acceptable to the more rational mindset of critical scholarship is an academic question. If we take the text on its own terms, prophecy – personal, political *and* predictive – is central to it.

Day 3

Overview: Daniel 2 and 7

Dreams of kings and prophets

Chapter 2 is set in the early years of the exile, and describes Daniel's first 'engagement' with King Nebuchadnezzar. The king has been disturbed by a vivid dream. Clearly it should mean something, but he doesn't know what, and all the wise men of Babylon can't tell him. The king, who holds the power of life and death over all his subjects, decrees that all the wise men will be killed unless an interpreter is found. This brings Daniel and his friends into the story, as Daniel takes the lead in averting certain death. Through prayer, he is able to discern both the dream and its meaning, and this he delivers to the king. The interpretation catapults Daniel's prophetic role to centre stage, because the dream proves to be a direct message from God for the king concerning the future of his reign. So convinced is Nebuchadnezzar of the interpretation offered that he pours honour on Daniel and his friends, and acknowledges Yahweh as 'God of gods'.

"Whatever reason we give, the concluding scene gives us a powerful picture that reinforces the theme of our book: The most powerful pagan in the world lies prostrate before an exiled Jew. Chills of excitement and the flames of hope will rise in the hearts of those who identify with Daniel and his God."
Tremper Longman[49]

Chapter 7 is set some sixty years later, in the reign of Belshazzar, who was the son of King Nabonidus and reigned in Babylon as his co-regent for ten years. The chapter in many ways parallels chapter 2. Here we are offered an account of Daniel's own dream, in which visions of the future are described.

- Nebuchadnezzar's earlier dream described four successive kingdoms in terms of the four sections of a great statue, and looked to a further, final kingdom that would overcome all others and last forever.

- Daniel's later dream also describes four kingdoms, this time as four beasts arising from the sea. Again a further, godly kingdom arises. This is an everlasting kingdom, superseding all others and offering security to the saints of God.

This later vision confirms the apocalyptic nature of the book of Daniel and introduces the five final chapters, which further explore this theme in a series of dramatic visions. But the clear parallels between the dreams of chapters 2 and 7 confirm that even in the 'story' elements of its first half, the book of Daniel is apocalyptic/prophetic in nature.

Tremper Longman III suggests that six major themes, introduced in the stories of Daniel 1–6, reverberate through the prophetic visions of Daniel 7–12.

- The horror of human evil, particularly as it is concentrated in the state.

- The announcement of a specific time of deliverance.

- Repentance that leads to deliverance.

- The revelation that a cosmic war stands behind human conflict.

- Judgement as certain for those who resist God and oppress his people.

- The equally certain truth that God's people, downtrodden in the present, will experience new life in the fullest sense.

Does Daniel see the future?

The issue of the predictive power of prophecy is unavoidable in considering Daniel. Even separating the 'stories' (chapters 1–6) from the 'visions' (chapters 7–12) doesn't resolve the problem, since the book's historical predictions are evident already in chapter 2. The four kingdoms predicted are generally assumed to fit well with the period from the sixth to second centuries BC, culminating in the attempts by Antiochus Epiphanes to wipe out the beliefs and practices of Judaism. It is for this reason, along with stylistic and contextual evidence, that the majority of scholars agree on a second century date for the final editing of Daniel, even if some of its material comes from an earlier period. But dating does not in itself solve the prophetic riddles of Daniel for several reasons.

- Regardless of date, there is a clear 'supernaturalism' to the book of Daniel. Certain details can be rationalised, but removing God's capacity to intervene in any and every circumstance and to speak clearly to those who have ears to hear him, leaves very little.

- Daniel's dreams and visions appear to be fulfilled in what we know of history from the sixth to the second centuries, but that accounts for only some of the detail. Particularly in chapters 2 and 7, there is clear reference to a further future kingdom so that even if Daniel was *entirely* composed in the second century it remains a prophetic, predictive book.

- This prophetic, predictive trait is confirmed by the New Testament's treatment of Daniel. Jesus presents his own identity and ministry in terms of Daniel's prophecies, both as fulfilled in his coming and as 'yet to be', and the book of Revelation clearly implies that aspects of Daniel's visions are yet to be fulfilled.

- Even if Daniel's prophecies are an example of 'inspired observation', enabling him to correctly discern and understand the cycles by which history so often repeats itself – a view accepted by a number of commentators – they remain uncannily predictive of the future. However Daniel is inspired, there is no question that he *is* inspired.

What can we learn from these prophecies?

For all the efforts made by successive generations to unlock the dramatic imagery of Daniel, the book does not present prophecy as a 'time and date' prediction of the actions of God in history. Much more importantly, it makes the theological assertion that behind history the purposes of God are being worked out. Like the book of Revelation, with its many references to Daniel's visions, the book of Daniel purports to lift the curtain on this invisible world of God's workings – with the clear aim of encouraging the people of God in times of trial. These dreams and visions remind us that:

- The purposes of God remain sure, even when they disappear from view.

- For those with ears to hear, and a heart willing to search, the plans of God can be discerned even at the most difficult of times.

- The promises of God are our source of hope. Hope is re-awakened when we are reminded of God's sovereignty and his plans for our world.

The response of the people of God to dreams and visions of this kind should not be to take out maps and diaries to plot the world's precise end, but rather to take courage in the assurance that the final scenes are already written, that the God who is sovereign over history guarantees love's victory over death. His kingdom *will* come and his will *will* be done, on earth as it is in heaven. In our exploration of the place of prophecy in Daniel, we will explore three key areas: *Prophecy as Perception, Prophecy as Political Engagement* and *Prophecy as Poetry and Song.*

Day 3

Teaching Block 1:
Prophecy as perception: inspired communication

1.1 Prophecy and Scripture
1.2 Prophecy and the church
1.3 Prophecy and evangelism
1.4 Prophecy and the future

"The 'wisdom' that is spoken of here in Chapter 2 is not something that can be attained by this kind of process [the observation of the patterns of life]. It is an insight given directly by God. It comes as an instantaneous revelation. It is, in fact, akin to the insight claimed by the Hebrew prophets." Ernest Lucas[50]

The term 'prophecy' can be used to describe a whole range of communication activities recorded in Scripture and experienced in the church. These can include:

- The **personal** – where dreams, visions, words and images are used to give direction and insight to a particular individual.

- The **predictive** – where themes and events in the future are brought alive in present experience.

- The **political** – where the plumbline of God's truth and justice is brought to bear on the political and social realities of the day.

- The **profound** – where inspired observations bring God's servants to a deeper understanding of the realities behind the events of history and of the everyday.

A number of key characteristics can be identified that make a lifestyle or proclamation prophetic, distinguishing it from the ordinary actions and communications of life. An action or communication is described as prophetic when it is:

- Inspired communication, making a vital link between today's experience and God's timeless truth.

"Most Christians will recall times when a word in a sermon, a song, a 'word of knowledge' or prophetic word has penetrated right down to the depths of their being. This might be called 'inspired communication', which is perhaps a useful simple definition of prophecy. When it happens, it's as if you are seen through, understood, and the secrets which no-one else knows are addressed and resolved by a word from someone who couldn't possibly have known what was in your heart." Graham Tomlin[51]

It is worth noting, though, that in the Old Testament the acid test of a prophecy's validity was in the objective evidence of history, not in the feelings of the recipient(s).

- It is 'go-between' communication, speaking of God to men and women and of men and women to God.

"A prophet is a human person who is admitted to Yahweh's cabinet and thus becomes another means of executing heaven's decisions on earth and a transmitter of messages between earth and heaven. This works both ways, for the prophet intercedes in the cabinet, speaking on earth's behalf there, as well as bringing announcements of heaven's decisions." John Goldingay[52]

- It is communication grounded more in God's invisible reality than in the everyday world visible to all.

"The prophets are not 'reasonable', accommodating themselves to what makes sense to us. They are not diplomatic, tactfully negotiating an agreement that allows us a 'say' in the outcome. What they do is haul us

unceremoniously into a reality far too large to be accounted for by our explanations and expectations. They plunge us into mystery, immense and staggering." Eugene Peterson[53]

- It is communication that moves the community towards God's plans and purposes, calling us to faithful obedience.

Prophecy is the means by which God speaks *through* people *to* people, by which we come to see the world as God sees it and by which the plans and purposes of God become real to us. It is *seeing*, *hearing* and *knowing* God's word for our world. Four important relationships mark out the healthy functioning of prophecy in the church: the relationships of prophecy to Scripture, to community, to evangelism and to hope.

1.1 Prophecy and Scripture:
The written word is the grounding of the spoken word

"Broadly construed, the language of the biblical text is prophetic: it anticipates and summons realties that live beyond the conventions of our day-to-day, take-for-granted world." Walter Brueggemann[54]

There is a foundational relationship between prophecy as God's *spoken* word and prophecy as God's *written* word. This is not merely a legal relationship, in which the written word is called upon to act as judge and referee when the spoken word seems too strange to believe; it is a nurturing, life-giving relationship. The prophet of the spoken word is shaped and formed by this relationship to the written word. The spoken word is *grounded in* the written word.

Daniel 9 offers an intriguing glimpse of this relationship. The chapter is an extended 'prophetic prayer', complete with angelic visitations and apocalyptic visions; but it is grounded in the study of Scripture. It is through his reading of the words of Jeremiah that Daniel is inspired to seek God's word for his day. The prophetic word in the sense of the immediate, God-given inspiration is grounded in the prophetic word in the sense of the established, God-given Scriptures.

"Daniel hears God's words in Jeremiah and responds through prayer. God then sends Gabriel

with yet further revelation. The principle is clear: ... God speaks to his people in his written and spoken word." Tremper Longman[55]

Old Testament scholar Craig Bartholomew insists on the importance of this relationship for all prophetic ministry.

"... a prophetic ministry – a ministry that brings God's word to bear on his people and his world – is founded on the authority of God's word. ... it is worth reminding ourselves that without a strong doctrine of the authority of Scripture as God's infallible word, we have no basis for a prophetic critique of our time and of our church." Craig Bartholomew[56]

It is as we are exposed to the ways in which God has spoken in the past, carried for us in Scripture, that we are inspired and empowered to hear God's word for our own day. The believer who longs to speak, on God's behalf, a dynamic, immediate word to a given context will be enabled to do so to the extent that he or she is immersed in God's written word. Just as Ezekiel was challenged to eat the scroll given to him, and only then to speak God's word to Israel (Ezek 3:1), it is as the prophet 'ingests' God's written word that he or she is able to speak out God's spoken word.

1.2 Prophecy and the church:
God's community is a sign of God's kingdom

"It is only in relation to Jesus Christ that we are transformed, becoming resident aliens whose very existence reveals that there is indeed an alternative on offer."
Graham McFarlane[57]

Because the word 'prophecy' is so closely linked to the word 'prophet', it is all too easy to think in exclusively individual terms. Prophets are often thought of as lone, and sometimes crazed, adventurers who live on locusts and talk in riddles. But in Scripture there is a deep and significant *communal* aspect to prophecy. It is *as a community* that the people of God are called to be his voice in the culture. Daniel spoke as one man, but he spoke *out of* his identity as a member of the Hebrew community. The church, like the nation of Israel before it, is called to be a *prophetic community* in the world.

- Pointing to the future that is carried in God's plans for the world.

"We believe that the church is called to be a sign, a foretaste and a herald of God's present but still emerging kingdom. Because the hallmark of that kingdom is God's reconciling work in the world, the church lives to point to, to embody, and to proclaim that reconciling work. ... If the church's embodied life and witness are to be a sign, a foretaste, and a herald of this kingdom, then the church must strive diligently to embody faithfully those convictions that make visible this kingdom." PD Kenneson and JL Street[58]

- Standing between God and the world.

"The church will always have to present itself both in the forum of God and in the forum of the world. For it stands for God to the world, and it stands for the world before God. It confronts the world in critical liberty and

is bound to give it the authentic revelation of the new life. At the same time it stands before God in fellowship and solidarity with all men and is bound to send up to him out of the depths the common cry for life and liberty." Jurgen Moltmann[59]

- Reminding the world of the life that is made possible in Christ.

"In every capital city, you can usually find communities of exiles. Chinese restaurants in San Francisco's Chinatown, Irish bars in Kilburn in London, Arab neighborhoods in Paris. In all of them, communities try to recreate the atmosphere of home, so that when you step inside you can begin to feel what it is like to be in the real country itself. There will be reminders that you aren't actually there yet. The weather in Paris is not always as warm as Saudi Arabia, and the road signs in Kilburn don't have their place names in Irish as they do in Dublin. However, these communities remind you of the real thing. They are also fairly good images of what the church is meant to be – a community that reminds others of the real thing; the kingdom of God; life under the rule of Christ. There will be reminders that this is not yet complete. Petty jealousies, envy and pride still rear their heads, yet the idea is that church is meant to be, as far as it can, a reminder of life under the rule of God." Graham Tomlin[60]

1.3 Prophecy and evangelism:
Provocative people call for a response

It is also important not to put 'prophecy' and 'evangelism' in two entirely separate boxes. The call on the church to *do* evangelism and the call to *be* prophetic are closely linked, and often overlap. Graham Tomlin suggests in *The Provocative Church* that it is by living out their prophetic calling that Christians will 'provoke' the evangelistic process and its response.

"Christians are not meant to just try and do good, be nice and help the world work a little better. They are instead to act as signposts to another order, another way of life, another kingdom, which can be glimpsed in this world but has not yet arrived completely. ... With a strong sense of Christian identity, Christians

can be encouraged simply to be their own Christian selves in front of their neighbours and work colleagues. As they work out with their fellow believers what it means to live under the rule of God, they are to live those lives publicly, never make a secret of the fact that they are Christians, and wait to see what happens." Graham Tomlin[61]

Walter Brueggemann also makes the important link between evangelism and prophecy. In *Biblical Perspectives on Evangelism: Living in a Three-Storied Universe,* he affirms that evangelism, like prophecy, must have at its heart the articulation of news that will otherwise be unheard.

"The noun 'gospel', which means 'message', is linked in the Bible to the verb 'tell-the-news' (one word, bissar, in Hebrew). At the center of the act of evangelism is the message announced, a verbal, out-loud assertion of something decisive not known until this moment of utterance. There is no way that anyone, including an embarrassed liberal, can avoid this lean, decisive assertion which is at the core of evangelism." Walter Brueggemann[62]

By both lifestyle and articulation, the church lives to 'announce' the reign of God, provoking those who have lived outside God's rule to ask the question, "What does this mean?"[63]

Health Warning: You have to be different to make a difference.

"For Western Christendom as a whole, then, the question comes to be defined thus: Has the acculturation of the churches to a culture shaped by fundamentally materialistic values resulted in the eclipsing of the authentic message of Christ, leaving believers incapable of pointing towards an alternative vision for the future of humankind and the world?" David Smith[64]

There is a simple assertion that runs through the book of Daniel like a golden thread, and is sometimes so obvious we are in danger of missing it: you have to be different to make a difference. There is no prophecy and no evangelism when the people of God are so absorbed into their surroundings that they have become invisible.

In the study of Information Theory, there is a basic definition that states that information is 'a difference that makes a difference'. Information is, firstly, a *difference* – there must be a mark or a symbol that stands out from its surroundings – black ink on a white page; tally marks scratched on a prison wall; hieroglyphics on the tomb of a king. But to be genuine information, this difference must *make a difference* – it must add something to the reader/receiver that he or she does not already know.

The same definition can be helpfully applied to God's people, whether we are dealing with the call to be a community in exile, delving into the role of the prophet or developing the church's evangelistic task. Whatever our context, we are called to be *the difference that makes a difference*.

1.4 Prophecy and the future:
Glimpses of tomorrow give meaning to today

The popular understanding of prophecy as 'telling the future' is limited and limiting, and does little to capture the biblical understanding of this important gift, but is not entirely false; prophecy does, very often, speak of the future. In the book of Daniel, in the wider witness of Scripture and in the historic experience of the church, *inspired communication* is often used to speak of future events. There can be no doubt, for example, that the earliest Christian communities described in the New Testament:

- Believed in Jesus as the fulfilment of much that God had spoken of predictively through the prophets of Israel.

- Believed that some of the events predicted by the prophets of Israel were yet to be fulfilled.

- Believed that God was still able to speak in words, dreams and visions of events yet to take place.

Both the written word of Scripture and the spoken word of the church's prophets are presented in the New Testament as having predictive power. This is seen to operate at three levels.

1. The preaching of the apostles is rich with references to prophecies that described, in advance, events fulfilled in Jesus and in the life of the church. The sermons of Peter in Acts 2 and 3, of Stephen in Acts 7 and of Paul in Acts 13 establish direct links between the writings of the prophets and the events surrounding the birth of the church.

2. Direct words are given to God's people in specific circumstances to enable them to discern God's will. The meeting of Philip with the Ethiopian eunuch (Acts 8), the role of

Day 3

Ananias in the conversion of Saul (Acts 9) and the introduction of Peter to Cornelius (Acts 10) are three examples.

3. The future, both immediate and distant, is described in such a way as to give hope, direction and courage to God's people. John's revelation on the island of Patmos is the stand-out example, but the 'futuring' of the faith is also a feature of the writings of Paul, for example in 1 Thessalonians, and of Peter (1 Pet 4, 2 Pet 3).

The centrality of prophecy to the New Testament should encourage us to immerse ourselves in the prophecies of God's written word, to be open to God's spoken word for our day, to understand our present circumstances in the light of both and to be ready to give a word of assurance and encouragement to our waiting world.

Health Warning: Prophecy is fuel for hope, not for hype.

Central to this predictive power of prophecy is the belief that the word of God brings hope. The core assertion of predictive prophecy in Scripture is that God is working out his purposes. This is particularly important in reading apocalyptic literature, with its disturbing images of beasts and battles. Apocalyptic literature uses dramatic visual images to speak of the end of the present age and the arrival of the age to come. Complex, rich in metaphor and often difficult to understand, the apocalyptic is written not to amuse and entertain but to give hope. God doesn't give prophets a glimpse of his plans for the world so they can take note of times and dates and score points for accurate

prophecy, but so that the people of God can take courage in their current situation however difficult it might be.

Apocalyptic, then, in common place parlance communicates an impending sense of doom, a feeling that existence might come to an end at any moment. With this popular understanding of the term we are getting closer to the biblical idea, but we are not quite there yet. A violent end to history is in the ultimate purview of biblical apocalyptic. However, far from imparting a sense of doom and pessimism, books like Daniel and Revelation radiate with joy and optimism. Why? Because the end is the end of human corruption and the oppression of God's people and is brought about by the audience's warring God. Apocalyptic celebrates God's victory over the enemies of the godly.[65]

In the book of Daniel there is a significant continuity between the *stories* of chapters 1 to 6, in which we see that God is in control despite appearances to the contrary, and the *visions* of chapters 7 to 12, which assert that God will remain in control and will ultimately overcome the evil forces of the day. What Daniel the exile *discovers* in his experience of the present, Daniel the prophet *describes* in his visions of the future. This helps us to understand the purpose of apocalyptic, which is to proclaim the future victory of God so that hope is birthed in present experience.

In The Zone

What might be the impact of prophecy as inspired communication on the specific Zone you are exploring?

- *Faith and a Changing World*
  How do the prophets of God's written word help us to understand the changes our culture is undergoing? What other 'prophetic voices' are speaking to us today?

- *Faith and the Developing World*
  In God's global family, under what circumstances can glimpsing the future victory of God bring hope to birth in present experience? What role does prophecy play in the growth of the church amongst the poor?

- *Faith and Devotional Life*
  How does prophecy interact with prayer and the devotional life? Is Daniel 9 a model of 'prophetic prayer'? What fresh prayers does it inspire for today?

- *Faith and Everyday Life*
  What is the role of prophecy in the church today? How can we be fully open to God's prophetic word in Scripture, in preaching and in worship?

- *Faith and Family Life*
  What is the place of prophecy in family life? Can God speak to us directly about our families and households? If the church is called to 'be the difference that makes a difference', what does this imply for family life?

- *Faith and Involvement*
  What is the place of inspired communication in public life? Is it possible to speak God's direct word in this context? How might glimpsing God's ultimate future victory change the way we engage in the realities of public life and service in the present?

- *Faith and Working Life*
  What might be the role of inspired communication in the workplace? Where does the prophetic nature of Scripture touch on our careers and working lives?

Question Time

The final statement of this teaching section suggests that prophecy is fuel for hope, not for hype. What positive examples can you bring

- Of the *written* prophecies of Scripture bringing a clear and relevant word of hope to a situation in which you have been involved?

- Of the *spoken* prophecy of a direct word from God bringing direction and encouragement in your experience?

- Of the language and images of apocalyptic literature bringing strength and encouragement to a community facing difficult circumstances?

Day 3

Teaching Block 2:
Prophecy as political engagement: calling leaders to account

2.1 The political prophet engages in both seeing and speaking
2.2 The political prophet brings together sacred and secular
2.3 The political prophet refuses both denial and despair
2.4 The political prophet pursues both intimacy and involvement

"Prophetic voices are those which read the signs of the times in the light of the justice and love of God, and speak out against all that distorts or diminishes the image of God in human beings." Kathy Galloway[66]

"Claiming that the Bible is a political book does not mean that it is party-political. The Bible focuses on 'the politics of God'. It does so because in its pages God reveals himself as the ultimate ruler – the King of kings. Consequently, one of the main themes of the Bible is the 'kingdom of God', which is crucial for our understanding of God, the church and civil society, including the role of the state." Roy McCloughry[67]

If the broad understanding of prophecy in Daniel is that of inspired communication, there is also a more specific sense in which this leads to political engagement. Both in his overall approach to exile, and in his specific dealings with the kings of Babylon, Daniel demonstrates that the call to be a prophetic voice in pagan culture includes a significant political dimension. This reflects the wider witness of Scripture, in which political engagement is a consistent and important aspect of the prophetic tradition. In particular, Daniel's relationship with Nebuchadnezzar, and later with Belshazzar, casts him in the role of the prophet who holds the king accountable before God.

"Beginning with Samuel in his relation with Saul (cf. 1 Sam 13,15), a major role of the prophet has been to serve as the conscience of the king." Tremper Longman[68]

Daniel's courage in adopting this role is significant, because he is in exile. He could have been forgiven for assuming that a prophet of

Israel would only be called upon to challenge a king of Israel. This had largely been the case to date, and made perfect sense in terms of God's covenantal law. The king was raised up by God *under* the covenant, and could therefore be held accountable by reference *to* the covenant. The prophets called those in power to return to faithfulness to the covenant from which their power was derived. But in Babylon, Daniel addresses kings who have no knowledge of Israel's covenant. Israel's history, Israel's law and Israel's God are of no interest to them. And yet Daniel insists that it is by God's permission that they rule, and by God's standards that they will be judged.

John Holdsworth, in *Dwelling in a Strange Land: Exile in the Bible and in the Church,* cites this change as a significant theological shift brought to the surface by the exile. Because of the exile, he suggests, the Hebrews became newly aware of three important theological ideas.

• God is the God of all creation

• God is the God of all history

• God is the God of all peoples.

These ideas are present in earlier Hebrew literature. They are suggested as far back as the call of Abraham, and are present in the commissioning of Moses. Not least, they shape the thinking of the prophets themselves. But it is the shock of the exile that brings them centre stage for many Hebrews. Daniel, in particular, takes the 'traditional' role of the prophet as one who calls a Hebrew king back to faithfulness to the covenant and extends the same call even to the Babylonian kings. Prophecy, then, ceases to be the means by which the God of Israel speaks through individuals to his covenant people – it becomes the means by which the God of creation speaks through individuals to all people.

The prophet is thus authorised to call all those

in political power to account on the basis of God's universal, creational laws of justice and righteousness. Key pairs of values can be said to mark out this political dimension of prophecy in Scripture and in the life of the church.

2.1 The political prophet engages in both seeing and speaking

At the heart of the political dimension of prophecy, there is a refusal to be silent – an insistence, under the authority of God, that it is right to speak out when injustice and unrighteousness are seen. Because prophecy is 'inspired communication' – because it is in essence about speaking out – its political dimension begins with speaking out against injustice. Kathy Galloway, poet, writer and leader of the Iona Community, describes the cost to the community when the church is unable or unwilling to speak God's word *into* the struggles and tensions of the world.

"A friend was a miner during the British miners' strike of the early 1980s. In this protracted and bitter conflict, which affected every home in the village, the minister did not once refer to any aspect of the strike in either preaching or prayer. The people of this community were left to struggle with almost unendurable realities bereft of any word of

wholeness from this official representative of the gospel. The word of life that saved them was ministered to them in the soup kitchens and the homes of the mostly unchurched. No wonder my friend felt betrayed by the church." Kathy Galloway[69]

It is as we see and perceive injustice in the world, and measure up the world *as it is* against the world *as God calls it to be,* that we must find the courage to speak out.

"We are the voice of prophecy to the world. We are to be uncompromising about all that is contrary to God's purposes, whether poverty, debt, slavery, moral evil or social decadence. Christians are therefore called to be the voice of prophecy, of resistance in an unjust society, and this may sometimes mean declaring that God is judge of the world. The church is not exempt from the impact of such declarations in its own life." Roy McCloughry[70]

2.2 The political prophet brings together sacred and secular

"Amidst our complex modern societies God calls his people still to bring a kingdom perspective to bear on the totality of their lives and to resist the idols of the day." Craig Bartholomew[71]

The political dimension of prophecy arises, in part, from the refusal to see life divided into neat categories of 'sacred' and 'secular' concerns. Prophets are called to speak to the political dimensions of life because all of life is subject to God's rule and to God's word.

"One of the bad habits that we pick up early in our lives is separating things and people into secular and sacred. We assume that the secular is what we are more or less in charge of: our jobs, our time, our entertainment, our government, our social relations. The sacred is what God has charge of: worship and the Bible, heaven and hell, church and prayers. We then contrive to set aside a sacred place for God, designed, we say, to honor God but really intended to keep God in his place, leaving us free to have the final say about everything

Day 3

else that goes on. Prophets will have none of this. They contend that everything, absolutely everything, takes place on sacred ground. ... Nothing is hidden from the scrutiny of God, nothing is exempt from the rule of God, nothing escapes the purposes of God. Holy, holy, holy." Eugene Peterson[72]

The call to the Christian community to abandon false dualisms and acknowledge the lordship of Christ over the whole of life is not a new call:

it has been repeated time and again to the church over the centuries, and often in recent years. But it is a call, so it seems, that we often struggle to receive: and the fear in the church of speaking and acting in the political arena is evidence of our failure to hear and heed it.

"This creation-wide, all-embracing perspective of prophetic ministry is absolutely crucial if we are to bring a critical perspective to bear upon our culture." Craig Bartholomew[73]

2.3 The political prophet refuses both denial and despair

"God abides in the realities of justice, love and freedom. He is not automatically present in pious words. If we do not include the realities of freedom, justice and love when we speak of God, then we are speaking of some ideal and not of the living God." Leonardo Boff[74]

Exploring the responses of the Hebrew exiles to life in Babylon, David Smith suggests that two equal and opposite dangers face a church in exile.

- The first is *insular traditionalism,* in which the experience of exile becomes "hardened into a liturgical tradition which marginalises praise and thanksgiving ... and involves a morbid remembrance of the tragedies which befell an earlier generation."

- The second danger is *cultural assimilation,* in which what once seemed like a strange and alien culture comes to be viewed as 'home', particularly by the generation who did not experience the journey from Jerusalem to Babylon.[75]

In simple terms, these options might be called respectively 'despair' and 'denial'. The first sees the state of the world as too terrible to contemplate, and is driven to a state of fear, incapable of action. There is lament for the condition

of the world, but its result is not engagement but escape. In the world of denial, by contrast, mourning has no place. Here the problems of the world go unnoticed, and no critique of the dominant culture is offered. Instead of challenging the evident evils of society, the church retreats into a safe, religious world of dull conformity. The biblical, prophetic alternative is faith that sees the realities of the day and yet has courage, that engages with real life in the real world because its hope is founded on God's purposes.

"Hebrews 11:1 says that faith is 'the substance of things hoped for and the evidence of things not seen'. The world is waiting for a people who will offer the value of hope. Hope that change is possible. Hope that inspires them to bet their lives on such change. My own paraphrase of Hebrews 11:1 is this: Hope is believing in spite of the evidence, and then watching the evidence change..." Jim Wallis[76]

Biblical social involvement is not motivated by the false hope that political action alone can change the world, but neither does it accept the view that change is impossible. Rather, it engages because by our actions, and the power of God at work, real change is possible.

2.4 The political prophet pursues both intimacy and involvement

Lastly, the political dimension of prophecy refuses to see action and engagement as an alternative to worship. A dynamic relationship with the world is not an alternative to a dynamic relationship with God – for the prophet the two belong together.

Steve Chalke, the founder of Oasis Trust and the Faithworks Movement, has characterised this important balance as the marriage of 'intimacy and involvement.'

"Intimacy with God and involvement with society are inseparably connected in Jesus' final words to his disciples as recorded by Matthew, 'Go...and surely I am with you always,' (Matt 28:19–20). So it is that the 'stay-at-home' church can never know the intimacy it so craves, for it is in the act of 'going' that we encounter the risen Jesus. True intimacy with God is the outcome of our involvement in his world. Involvement in God's world is the outcome of genuine intimacy. Intimacy and involvement belong together – to ignore one is always to destroy the quality and depth of the other." Steve Chalke[77]

This balance means that the believer is not forced to choose between work and worship, nor between prayer and politics. As is evident in the life of Daniel, prophetic, God-inspired words and actions arise from a life of deep devotion to prayer and discipline. The dry-as-dust activist who knows the answer to all the world's problems but is not nourished with the very life of God has no place in prophetic political action – and neither has the spiritual space cadet who regularly scales the dizzy heights of devotion but rarely sets foot in the real world. Contemplative activists; prayerful politicians; worshipful workers – these are the balanced believers the world so desperately needs. It is those who have found the secrets both of *being* and of *doing* who will most impact and change their world for the better.

"We have been so programmed to believe that being a Christian witness is to be frenetic for Jesus. But the greatest witness we can be is to be. It's being there with our values and lifestyle which makes our words authentic. It is to live curious lives which make people ask, 'Why?' When we lose confidence in that truth we are likely to panic into excessive words and activities designed to prove that we are Christians. ... Daniel is an excellent biblical model of prophetic presence in the workplace. His prophetic witness was not just in his prayer life or his ability to interpret and predict future events. He also showed us that prophetic conduct includes a faultless professionalism as a senior diplomat." Joel Edwards[78]

Health Warning: You don't have to be precious to be provocative.

In a historical review of the ways in which the evangelical churches have engaged with social and political concerns, David Bebbington points out how easily an unhelpful understanding of 'provocation' can take over.

"The evangelical style of engagement with the ills of society has encountered a number of risks. One has been the danger of clamour. A bellicose tone, an inflated rhetoric and exaggerated charges have often marked the campaigns. At the end of the nineteenth century a number of non-conformist ministers, dedicated to what they deemed Christian goals, fell into this trap. In particular Hugh Price Hughes, the leading Wesleyan activist, habitually engaged in furious tirades against opponents, whether publicans, Catholics or Prime Ministers. A contemporary called him 'a Day of Judgement in breeches'. ... Apart from tactical considerations, there is the problem that a hectoring tone is a poor advertisement for Christianity. A militant moralism rarely reflects the meekness, the kindness and the longsuffering reflected in Scripture. Few aspects of evangelical religion have done more to deter converts than the stridency of the popular campaigns it has mounted." David Bebbington[79]

Day 3

Contrast this with the life of Daniel. In Daniel 2:14 Arioch, the captain of the king's guard, is sent to kill Daniel, and all the wise men of Babylon. Daniel, we are told, 'spoke to him with wisdom and tact'. The ultimate result is that the lives of Daniel, his Hebrew friends *and* his pagan colleagues are saved: and we are introduced to a way of operating that will be consistent through Daniel's long career in Babylon. Though the rulers that Daniel faces are pagan kings who have robbed the Hebrews of their home and heritage, they nonetheless deserve to be approached with tact and wisdom.

Commenting on this same incident in Daniel's life, Ajith Fernando writes:

"I have a friend who is a pastor in a Muslim country. He has often had threats on his life because of his evangelistic activity. One day a group of twenty fanatical, young Muslims came to his house and angrily demanded that he come out. My friend came out realising that he was at death's door. While his wife prayed inside, he spoke politely to the youths, offered them chairs to sit on and said he would like to discuss with them their cause for agitation. They angrily refused to talk to him. He offered to bring them some tea to drink, in keeping with the way visitors are treated in our part of the world. Again they angrily refused.

With these youths was a learned Muslim scholar. He called the boys to himself and told them to contrast their behaviour with that of the Christian pastor. He told them how rude they had been to the pastor (clergy of all religions are usually treated with much respect in the East). Then he reminded them of how polite the pastor had been, of how he had offered them chairs to sit on and tea to drink. He told them that they should be ashamed of themselves, and he asked each to apologise to the pastor. This they did, each one individually, after which they quietly departed. ... When we live for Christ in a world that is hostile to his ways, we will often face situations that ordinarily would cause us to panic or to lash back excitedly. But what is needed *at such times is wisdom and tact. Daniel was zealous for God and his principles. But along with his zeal he had wisdom that caused him to be tactful in sensitive situations."*[80]

Whether dealing with the broader political issues of the day or confronting specific personal issues, Daniel holds out the hope that it is possible to be both provocative and polite – to be obedient without being obnoxious. This does not mean that a prophetic life will never bring conflict. The furnace and the lions' den are ample evidence that it will. But it does mean that those who claim to be the voice of God must also evidence the character of God.

Question Time

This teaching block has suggested that a foundational theological lesson of the exile is the triple discovery that *God is the God of all creation*, that *God is the God of all history* and that *God is the God of all peoples*. How does this triple assertion impact:

- The way believers relate to those in power and authority who do not share their faith and beliefs?

- The basis on which Christians engage in political and social action?

- The kinds of issues about which believers might want to be vocal, protest, campaign and raise public concern?

In The Zone

In the Zone you are exploring consider the impact of four pairs of values, described above as characteristic of prophetic political engagement: engaging in both seeing and speaking; bringing together the sacred and the secular; refusing both denial and despair; and pursuing both intimacy and involvement.

- *Faith and a Changing World*
  How does seeing and speaking relate to the changes that are sweeping through our culture? How are denial and despair evident in the church's response to a time of change in society?

- *Faith and the Developing World*
  How does the need for seeing and speaking about injustice change when we take on a global rather than a national perspective? How does the pursuit of both intimacy and involvement play out in the diversity of God's global family?

- *Faith and Devotional Life*
  How does the bringing together of sacred and secular concerns impact the devotional life? Is the balance of intimacy and involvement a realistic aim, or an unreachable and unsustainable goal?

- *Faith and Everyday Life*
  What is the place of prophetic political action in the church today? Is it up to specific individuals to see and speak about injustice, or should the church have a corporate voice? What might the refusal of both denial and despair mean for the worship life of our churches?

- *Faith and Family Life*
  Is there a place in family life for seeing and speaking about political matters? What actions can families and households take to nurture a balance of intimacy and involvement?

- *Faith and Involvement*
  How might the overcoming of the divisions between sacred and secular help the church to support those engaged in public service? What are the challenges facing those engaged in public service in seeking to balance intimacy with involvement?

- *Faith and Working Life*
  How might the call for prophecy as seeing and speaking impact the believer in the workplace? What implications does the bringing together of sacred and secular have for the way in which believers conduct their working lives? Is the refusal of both denial and despair a relevant choice in the workplace?

Voices from Exile:

Steve Chalke – The power of compromise

The interviewer's question was straight to the point. 'Do you ever find that your involvement in public life and media means that you end up having to compromise?' The problem was that I couldn't give the firm and reassuring 'of course not' answer that I knew so many in my audience were hoping for. In truth, my whole life is a constant succession of compromises. I'm caught in an endless tension. I find myself torn between what I would like to do, say, see happen, and commit to, and at the same time having to work within the restriction of budgets (and in some cases the law); keep prior commit-

ments; meet existing responsibilities; deal with conflicting priorities; and slowly learn that the best way to win ground is to choose my battles with care.

When I was taught the story of Daniel as a child the point, as far as my teachers were concerned, could not have been clearer. Here was one of God's heroes who, however intense the pressure, would never even contemplate compromise. To use the words of Martin Luther from an era yet to come, 'Here I stand, I can do none other'. But in truth the real story of Daniel

Day 3

is far more complex than that. Daniel was a Jew who wanted to live in Jerusalem not Babylon. He dreamt of being in the service of the royal house of David not that of Nebuchadnezzar. He longed to be part of a society governed by the law of Yahweh, but instead was a civil servant within a pagan culture based on a value system far different from his own. In short, he was required to live, work and serve within a strange environment which impinged on his freedom, lifestyle and choices at all levels.

Compromise turns out to be the very air that Daniel had to breathe each day. Rather than a man who knew 'no compromise', he was one who had to learn when to compromise and when to stand his ground. Nor is the book of Daniel a 'quick reference guide' spelling out the exact *what and when* of where to draw the line for twenty-first century Christians. Its purpose is very different. First, its message is that all those who wish to live their lives God's way, within any alien culture, will inevitably find themselves in conflict with it at various points. But secondly, it calls all God's people to do the hard work of wrestling with what it

means to live out authentic biblical faith in their culture and context. For us, Daniel therefore poses the vital question of what following Jesus and being distinctively Christian looks like in the strange world of post-Christendom and then leaves us the challenge of rising to the moment?

Though the book of Daniel tells us explicitly about where Daniel and his three friends chose to draw the line – it does not inform us of the many discussions they must have had over points of tension between their faith and Babylon's culture where they eventually decided either not to make a stand, or that the time wasn't yet right.

Likewise, I explained to my interviewer, I frequently find myself in the same kind of situations, facing the struggle to know which battles to fight and which to let go; praying for the wisdom to know when and where to draw the line and for the courage to make a stand, whatever the cost, at the right time over the right issues. Or to put it another way, learning how to sing the Lord's song in a strange land.

Voices From Exile:
The Micah Network

In September 1999 a small group of evangelical leaders from non-governmental relief and development organisations met in Kuala Lumpur, Malaysia, to create a new global network for Christian social transformation. The core aims of the network were defined as:

- Making a 'biblically shaped response' to the needs of the poor and oppressed'.

- Speaking strongly and effectively regarding the mission of the church to proclaim and demonstrate the love of Christ to a world in need.

- Prophetically calling upon and influencing the leaders and decision-makers of societies to maintain the rights of the poor and oppressed and rescue the weak and needy.

This new initiative, named the Micah Network, will work in the different regions of the world

to coordinate the work of Christian churches and agencies and to campaign jointly on key social and economic issues. Its core values are represented in the *Declaration on Integral Mission*, posted at www.micahnetwork.org, which states.

"It is not simply that evangelism and social involvement are to be done alongside each other. Rather, in integral mission our proclamation has social consequences as we call people to love and repentance in all areas of life. And our social involvement has evangelistic consequences as we bear witness to the transforming grace of Jesus Christ. If we ignore the world we betray the word of God which sends us out to serve the world. If we ignore the word of God we have nothing to bring to the world. Justice and justification by faith, worship and political action, the spiritual and the material, personal change and structural change belong together. As in the life of Jesus,

being, doing and saying are at the heart of our integral task."[81]

Commenting on the use of the prophet Micah in this context, Joe Kapolyo has written that:

"The name Micah holds before us a biblical mirror showing why we get involved with the needy. Micah, after all, presents a searing prophetic account of social injustice in Judah prior to the reforms of Hezekiah. Micah's analysis is that of a prophet who hailed from the relatively impoverished rural fringes of Jewish society. He offers a penetrating description of the empty ritualism, corruption, greed, injustice and other social ills of the day, especially as they affected the small towns and villages of Judah. As such, he provides a grid through which Christians today might attempt to deal authentically with the inequality, exploitation and misery of so many in our own world."[82]

Voices From Exile:
Jim Wallis – The Lord's song in Sing Sing

There's a lot of talk where I come from, in the USA, about the Faith-Based Initiative. It's the big issue for The White House, for Democrats and Republicans. I teach at Harvard part-time, and even up there most of us didn't know that we were FBOs – faith-based organisations – until a couple of years ago. We were just church folks in the streets, in the trenches. Now, according to the president, we're FBOs. So we've had these conversations with him and others.

But my notion of it all doesn't really derive from the halls of power, or from academia, as important as those places are. It derives, rather, from an invitation I received a couple of years ago from the inmates at Sing Sing prison, in upstate New York.

The inmates there said, "Would you come and speak to us?"

I thought this was a good idea, so I wrote back and told them I would. "When would you like me to come?" I asked.

They said, "We're free most nights. We're kind of a captive audience!"

The prison officials were very generous: they gave us a room in the bowels of the prison, way back underneath, and 75 men and I spent about four hours together. I'll never forget what one of them said to me that night. He said, "All of us are from about four or five neighbourhoods in New York City: the whole prison, just about five neighbourhoods. It's like a train begins in my neighbourhood and that train ends up here, at Sing Sing prison."

"When I get out", he said, "I want to go back and stop that train."

That inmate had a conversation inside the walls of Sing Sing. Two years later, I was in New York City speaking at a town meeting, and guess who was up front? That young brother was leading a town meeting in New York City. Last month we honoured him at a banquet in Washington, DC, with what is known as the Amos Award – a way of recognising those from humble beginnings, sheep and goat herders, who become prophets of justice. When those on the very bottom of society can have that kind of faith – a faith that can stop trains or move mountains – well, that's what I call a faith-based initiative.[83]

Voices in Exile:
The humble teapot

(Using figures derived from the UK government publication *Social Trends* (HMSO, 2003), Tim Chester has devised a unique measure of the challenge to social involvement found on the doorstep of Britain's average local church.)

Perhaps the most powerful tool in Christian social involvement, a tool with the potential to make a huge impact on our communities, is the humble teapot. Let me explain. Within a short walk of the average town church in the UK there are likely to be 10,000 people, including:

- 1,200 people living alone, 580 of whom will be of pensionable age
- 1,500 people who talk to their neighbours less than once a week
- 50 people who have been divorced within the last year
- 375 single parents
- 18 pregnant teenagers
- 150 recent or contemplated abortions
- 250 people who are unemployed
- 1,700 people living in low income households
- 1,100 people with some kind of mental disorder
- 100 bereavements within the last year
- 2,700 people living in households without a car
- 60 people in a residential care home
- 1,280 people caring for a sick, disabled or elderly relative or friend
- 2,800 people who have been victims of crime in the past year
- 40 homeless people

- 15 asylum seekers

The striking thing about these statistics is how many of these problems can be met in some measure by simple human contact. It can simply involve sharing a cup of tea. A Christian friend of mine was talking with a social worker in a poor area of London. This social worker is a Marxist, so he has no particular sympathy for Christianity. My friend asked him whether the church made much of an impact in the community in which he worked.

The social worker said: "If you mean the public face of the church – its pronouncements, its projects and its initiatives – then the answer is resoundingly no. But if you took away all the kindnesses and neighbourly acts that Christians do – visiting the sick, shopping for the housebound and so on – then this community would fall apart."

Community involvement need not involve big projects with local authority funding. What counts is ordinary Christians with commitment and compassion.[84]

Teaching Block 3:
Prophecy as poetry: creative God – creative gospel

3.1 Poetry is a language of lament
3.2 Poetry is a language of imagination
3.3 Poetry is a language of metaphor and image
3.4 Poetry is the language of praise
3.5 Poetry is the language of Jesus

"When I was a child and summer holidays came around, our family would usually pack up the car, catch a ferry, and drive to the west of Ireland. My sister and I would often sleep in the back seat as we drove across Kilkenny, Tipperary and Limerick, and wake up as we entered the small town in County Clare where we would spend the next weeks lazily on holiday with family and friends. The west coast of Ireland is a wild and bracing place. As we arrived, we would usually walk out onto the rocks by the sea, or onto one of the various headlands nearby. All the stuffiness of hot cities and dull roads would be swept away as we stood looking into the great Atlantic Ocean, with the wind whipping our faces and the spray reaching up from the pounding waves far below to cling to our hair, leaving the taste of fresh salt air lingering in our mouths. There was exhilaration as the powerful and cleansing wind blew away all the dull memories of school and city streets. There was a touch of danger, as we peered over the cliffs to the turmoil of the sea far below. There was a delicious sense of anticipation as the long weeks of the summer stretched out before us. It was a world where we felt more alive and alert to everything happening around us – a

world of wonder, not exactly safe and predictable, but exhilarating and energising.

"Those childhood experiences give me an echo of what it means to enter into God's kingdom. Jesus ushered people into a new world. He invited people to enter the kingdom of God, the place where God is King, and his will is done. It, too, is a bracing world, not safe and predictable, but an exhilarating place where our deepest and best desires are met and where we find the love, forgiveness, significance and challenge we desperately crave. It is the kingdom in which Jesus Christ is king, and where we can find ourselves refreshed, elated, even trembling with anticipation."[85]

This evocative passage from Graham Tomlin's book *The Provocative Church* is an excellent contemporary reminder of the power of poetic language to communicate truth. The vivid images of childhood holidays – the pounding waves and the cleansing wind, the delicious anticipation of the summer days ahead – will do more for many readers to evoke the reality of God's kingdom than several pages of theological 'facts'. What is more, a passage like this does more than evoke the kingdom – it makes it attractive. There is an invitation in such language that propositions, no matter how powerful, cannot match. The third assertion about prophecy that emerges from the story of Daniel, and is held up throughout the scriptural witness, is that prophecy is better described as poetry than as prose.

"God needs prophets in order to make himself known, and all prophets are necessarily artistic. What a prophet has to say can never be said in prose."[86]

This has been a major emphasis in the work of Walter Brueggemann, where the term 'poetry' is used to describe a creative, intriguing and compelling form of communication, against the flat and factual delivery of 'prose'.

"To address the issue of a truth greatly reduced requires us to be poets that speak against a prose world*. The terms of that phrase are readily misunderstood. By prose I refer to a word that is organised in settled formulae, so that even pastoral prayers and*

love letters sound like memos. By poetry, I do not mean rhyme, rhythm, or metre, but language that moves like Bob Gibson's fast ball, that jumps at the right moment, that breaks open old worlds with surprise, abrasion and pace."[87]

In Scripture, poetry is very often the chosen language in which discourse about God is conducted – not only in the prophets but in aspects of the historic books, in the Psalms, in the Wisdom tradition and in the teaching style of Jesus. Poetry in this sense includes the language of parable and proverb, of psalm and song: it is communication in which words are released to dance in their raw and ragged beauty; in which images are left unexplained and metaphors undefined; in which there is room for intimacy and for intrigue, for delight and for discovery.

"The narrator of the Daniel story is a poet. He is not didactic. He neither scolds nor urges. He only proposes and imagines another way in the world." Walter Brueggemann[88]

Poetic forms are used in Scripture not to simplify its message but to add to its power; not just to make memorising easier but to make meaning deeper. Where facts bruise and batter, poetry entices and invites. The prophets serve as a graphic and unavoidable reminder that poetry is a language of surprise, of newness.

"Then perchance comes the power of poetry – shattering, evocative speech that breaks fixed conclusions and presses us always toward new, dangerous, imaginative possibilities." Walter Brueggemann[89]

But newness and surprise are not the only functions of prophetic (poetic) communication.

Day 3

3.1 Poetry is a language of lament

There are times when the people of God cannot move forward until they are able to lament – when mourning is the unavoidable route to re-joicing. This was true for the Hebrew exiles, and it is in the language of poetry that their lament is expressed (Psa 137, Lam 1–5, Isa 40–55).

"The songs of Zion were not mere folk survivals that could be detached from the covenantal worldview within which they were embed-ded. Rather, for a people in exile they were painful reminders of what had been lost and it was impossible to sing them in a situation in which the whole of experienced reality seemed to make a mockery of covenant faith. Such anguished cries of lament begin to reso-nate for Western Christians in the twenty-first century in a way that they never did, and perhaps never could, during the long era of

Christian dominance that has now come to an end." David Smith[90]

Hope comes to birth when loss is squarely faced, and it takes an artistic language, with mean-ings deeper than words alone can capture, to articulate the losses we may feel. "If our fathers and mothers had not sat and wept in Babylon by the canals (see Psalm 137 and Lamentations), there could have been no poet to say 'Comfort, comfort my people' (Isa 40:1). The very struc-ture of the gospel is an argument that pain felt and articulated in God's heart permits new pos-sibilities in the historical process ..."[91]

What situations might we face – situations of loss and bereavement, or of grief and mourning – in which only the language of lament can take us forward?

3.2 Poetry is a language of imagination

"The prophet engages in futuring fantasy. The prophet does not ask if the vision can be implemented, for questions of implementation are of no consequence until the vision can be imagined. The <u>imagination</u> must come before the <u>implementation</u>. ... It is the vocation of the prophet to keep alive the ministry of imagination." Walter Brueggemann[92]

Key to the role of prophecy in Scripture is that it opens up rather than closes down the imagination. The result of prophecy is that we have more possibilities, not fewer. We are more open, not less, to God's interventions and ac-tions. The language of prophecy, in this sense, unlocks possibilities: it broadens rather than narrows our horizons. It is for this reason that the prophets are at their most imaginative in

the situations that are the most desperate – in exile and imprisonment, in longing and loss. It is when the hope of God's intervention seems most shut down that the language of prophecy is most used to open up God's people to their future. There is no place quite like a cul-de-sac, with no way out, to show the imaginative power of prophetic (poetic) communication.

"If God can do more than we can ask or imag-ine, why not ask for more imagination?" Dan Davison asks, referring to Ephesians 3:20

What impact might the church have on con-temporary culture if its communication style was known to open up rather than shut down imagination?

3.3 Poetry is a language of metaphor and image

Tremper Longman's commentary on Daniel explores the importance of metaphor to the language of apocalyptic – a significant element in biblical prophecy.

"To get right to the point, apocalyptic is a metaphor-rich genre. In this regard it is like poetry. Metaphors and similes teach by anal-ogy. They throw light on difficult concepts

and things by relating them to something we know from common experience. As such, images speak truly and accurately, but not precisely. We often do not know where the analogy stops. In this way, images preserve mystery about ideas that are ultimately beyond our comprehension. It is a travesty, then, to interpret apocalyptic images too finely, to press them in their details. As we will see, this mistake is common among biblical interpreters of apocalyptic and has led to all kinds of fanciful interpretations and outlandish claims. Caution and reserve are virtues in the interpretation of apocalyptic." Tremper Longman[93]

Poetry and prophecy alike are empowered by the need to *evoke* rather than *describe*. They thrive on moving the reader or listener to begin a journey, rather than complete it, and for this reason are more reliant on the suggestive power of images than the precise meanings of words.

Ernest Lucas suggests that apocalyptic literature in particular is rich in imagery. "The striking thing about Daniel 2 and 7 is the use of imagery that was deeply rooted in the culture of the eastern Mediterranean world," he writes. "Such imagery 'resonates' with people in ways that go beyond the purely rational. This use of deeply rooted cultural imagery is an important aspect of communication which Christians would do well to try to emulate today in communicating the gospel."[94]

What deeper riches of the spiritual journey become available to us when we open our lives to an encounter with God the image-maker, God the artist, God the poet?

3.4 Poetry is the language of praise

The Psalms, possibly the world's best-loved hymn book, remind us that poetry is very often the only language in which God's praise can be adequately expressed.

"In the Psalms we drink divine praise at its pure and stainless source, in all its primitive sincerity and perfection. We return to the youthful strength and directness with which the ancient psalmists voiced their adoration for the God of Israel." Thomas Merton[95]

Henri Nouwen discovered, while living and praying for several months in the silence of a Trappist monastery, a source of incomparable strength and sustenance in the memorisation and repetition of the Psalms. He later described the poetry of these ancient words.

"Slowly these words enter into the centre of my heart. They are more real than ideas, images, comparisons: they become a real presence. ... Many times I have thought if I am ever sent to prison, if I am ever subjected to hunger, pain, torture or humiliation, I hope and pray that they let me keep the Psalms. ... How happy are those who no longer need books but carry the Psalms in their heart

wherever they are and wherever they go." Henry Nouwen[96]

For Walter Brueggemann, prophecy, poetry and praise are all inter-linked in the God-inspired word that is spoken into our culture and context.

"We have only the word, but the word will do. It will do because it is true that the poem shakes the empire, that the poem heals and transforms and rescues, that the poem enters like a thief in the night and gives new life, fresh from the word and from nowhere else. There are many pressures to quiet the text, to silence this deposit of dangerous speech, to halt this outrageous practice of speaking alternative possibility. The poems, however, refuse such silence. They will sound. They sound through preachers who risk beyond prose. In the act of such risk, power is released, newness is evoked, God is praised." Walter Brueggemann[97]

Does the poetic richness, the depth and presence of the Psalms also run through our contemporary lives of prayer and worship? What new 'fields of praise' might open up before us if they did?

Day 3

3.5 Poetry is the language of Jesus

Finally, it is important to note that a prophetic (poetic) form of discourse is often evident in the teaching style of Jesus.

"Jesus' parables stand as witness that the kingdom comes by imagination, by poetic discourse. ... Jesus' way of teaching through parables was such a pastoral act of prophetic imagination in which he invited his community of listeners out beyond the visible realities of Roman law and the ways in which Jewish law had grown restrictive in his time." Walter Brueggemann[98]

In his book *Jesus Asked: What He Wanted to Know* Conrad Gempf explores in considerable depth the parabolic and questioning style of communication that dominates the public proclamations of Jesus. He likens this prophetic (poetic) communication to a puzzle or riddle.

"A riddle is, then, a figure of speech that wants some figuring out, usually by lateral thinking. And this is exactly what's going on in Jesus' parables. But in Jesus' case, they are not mere jokes or puzzles and not only told for their entertainment value. They are told to make a point – to teach – but they might do so in this roundabout sideways-thinking way." Conrad Gempf[99]

How differently might the world receive the message of the church if it always carried with it this questioning, inviting, mesmerising style of Jesus himself?

Prophetic (poetic) communication speaks more often through questions and riddles than through answers, more forcefully through images and metaphors than through facts. It prods and provokes, but does not pressurise. It entices and invites, but does not coerce. It deals in delight more fluently than dogma. It celebrates the beauty and the bounty of God, but seeks neither to measure his mystery nor to contain his creativity. It refuses to crate up and catalogue the truth and never declares the search complete. It is attractive, appetising, appealing and alive – and it always leaves you wanting more.

What revolutions might the global family of God experience if this were the mark of our every interaction with the world?

"Our words will seek to be servants of mystery, not removers of it as they were in the old world. They will convey a message that is clear yet mysterious, simple yet mysterious, substantial yet mysterious. My faith developed in the old world of many words, in a naïve confidence in the power of many words, as if the mysteries of faith could be captured like fine-print conditions in a legal document and reduced to safe equations. Mysteries, however, cannot be captured so precisely. Freeze-dried coffee, butterflies on pins and frogs in formaldehyde all lose something in our attempts at capturing, defining, preserving and rendering them less jumpy, flighty or fluid. In the new world, we will understand this a little better." Brian McLaren[100]

Question Time

This teaching block has suggested that prophetic (poetic) communication "provokes and prods but does not pressurise". Is this true in your reading of Scripture? If so, how might adoption of the same style and values impact:

- The methods and ideas we use to communicate the gospel in contemporary culture?

- The ways in which we teach the faith to believers, including children and young people?

- The approach we take to the questions and doubts that believers and unbelievers both bring, very often, to matters of faith?

In The Zone

What might the adoption of a prophetic (poetic) communication style mean to the Zone you are exploring?

- *Faith and a Changing World*
  In the changes taking place across our culture, will a prophetic (poetic) style be more needed tomorrow than today, or less? If it is more needed, what are the implications for our churches?

- *Faith and the Developing World*
  Does prophetic (poetic) communication as the language of lament have something to offer to God's global family? What insights do non-Western forms of communication bring to the assessment given above of the teaching style of Jesus.

- *Faith and Devotional Life*
  How can the poetry of the Psalms more fully shape and inform our devotional life as believers? Is the memorising of Scripture an old-fashioned idea we can happily live without, or a lost art we may need to re-discover?

- *Faith and Everyday Life*
  What difference might a more prophetic (poetic) language make to our experience of worship and praise? Is there a place in the church for newly written, contemporary psalms?

- *Faith and Family Life*
  What is the place of poetry and parable in the life of the family? In teaching and discipling our children, what matters more; to open them up to wonder, or to pass on to them the facts of the gospel?

- *Faith and Involvement*
  Is there a place for prophetic (poetic) discourse in public life? What part might the Psalms and Prophets, the Wisdom tradition and the teachings of Jesus play in shaping and resourcing the rhetoric of public service in today's culture?

- *Faith and Working Life*
  In terms of the contrasting definitions offered above, is the world of work in the UK today more an experience of prose ("a world that is organised in settled formulae") or poetry ("that breaks open old worlds with surprise, abrasion and pace")? What can believers do to make a difference?

Day 3

Conclusion:
The invitation home

Writing in the context of contemporary church life in America, Walter Brueggemann suggests that the poetic nature of prophecy is directly linked to the theme of exile:

"The poet in exile sings his people to homecoming. And that is a theme to which the exiled church in America is now summoned. The gospel is that we may go home. Home is not here in the consumer militarism of a dominant value-system. Home is also not in heaven, as though we may escape. Home, rather, is in

God's kingdom of love and justice and peace and freedom that waits for us. The news is we are invited home."[101]

Daniel was a prophet and poet, a preacher and a politician – and in each of these roles he sang the Lord's song *to* a people in exile and *on behalf of* a people in exile. So are we called, as prophets and poets, as preachers and politicians, to sing God's song in our exile; calling a people lost in Babylon to the true homecoming that is the kingdom of God?

Voices in Exile:
Let your kingdom come

Let it break out like blisters
On the skin of this city
Let it cut to the heart, like cardiac surgery
Let it flow into more lives than water fluoridation
Let it seep across more borders
Than Chernobyl's radiation

Let it blow in like a hurricane
Like a river, like a fire,
Let it spread like a virus, like a rumour, like war
Like the raising of a curtain, like the roll of a drum
Let it come to us: let your kingdom come

Let its landing be more welcomed than the Dalai Lama's jet
Let it touch more homes and households than the rise of credit debt
Let it be prized as a possession, like a ball signed by Babe Ruth
Let it take more liberties with hate than the tabloids take with truth
Let it hit the road more readily than Eddie Stobart's trucks
Let it show up in more suburbs than Blockbuster and Starbucks

Let it be beamed into more bedrooms
Than Popstars and Big Brother
Let it turn more heads in public
Than Brooklyn Beckham's mother

Let it blow in like a hurricane
Like a river, like a fire,
Let it spread like a virus, like a rumour, like war
Like the raising of a curtain, like the roll of a drum
Let it come to us: let your kingdom come

Let it sing a softer love song
Than Chris de Burgh's red lady
Let it blast out through more ghettoes
Than Eminem's Slim Shady
Let it win more public plaudits than the acting of Tom Cruise
Let it hold out hope for longer than Disney's theme-park queues
Let it pack more power potential than a phone box with Clark Kent in
Let it set more captives free than a breakout at San Quentin

Let it overturn more social norms
Than Marge and Homer's Bart
Let it be driven to more victories
Than Tiger Woods' golf cart

Let it blow in like a hurricane
Like a river, like a fire,
Let it spread like a virus, like a rumour, like war
Like the raising of a curtain, like the roll of a drum
Let it come to us: let your kingdom come[102]

Voices in Exile:
Brian McLaren – Communicating conviction

A few years ago I was invited by a friend to speak to a group of visiting scholars from the People's Republic of China. I was asked to speak on the existence of God. The lecture took place at the University of Maryland, where I used to teach English before I became a minister full time. These scholars had been through the Cultural Revolution, and then had experienced the Chinese version of *Glasnost,* and then had felt their world tighten again after the Tiananmen Square incident. I imagine it must have taken some courage to attend a lecture on this topic. But the attendance was good – about forty, as I remember.

Rather than argue for the existence of God, I felt I should take a different approach. I titled my lecture, "How to Think about the Existence of God". Instead of arguing for the existence of God, I presented a series of questions one would naturally need to consider in the search for God, with a kind of tree diagram to illustrate possible answers to each question. I tried to be somewhat objective and give each option a fair hearing, and then I explained which answers I had chosen in my own life, working my way down the tree diagram to the Christian faith. I also shared a personal story of how my faith had helped me deal with a difficult personal experience, when my son was diagnosed with leukaemia. I told them I hoped these thoughts had been helpful, and then opened the floor for questions.

A distinguished gentleman stood, with Asian respect, to ask his question: "Sir, I do not have a question, but I wish to thank you on behalf of all of us. You have helped us a great deal. Instead of telling us what you believe, you have told us how to believe, and this is very good for us."

Than a woman stood and said, "Yes, I agree with my colleague. You see, in my country, whenever anyone tells us what to believe, we know he is lying. The harder he pushes, the more we disbelieve him. Your approach is very helpful for us." From that point on, the evening flowed with some of the most honest and perceptive questions I have ever heard about faith.[103]

Day 3

Voices in Exile:
Books to read in Babylon

The work of Walter Brueggemann has made an enormous contribution to the contemporary understanding of the theme of exile in Scripture and of the wider significance of the prophetic writings. *The Prophetic Imagination* (Fortress Press, 1978) is a foundational treatment of the role of the prophet. *Hopeful Imagination: Prophetic Voices in Exile* (Fortress Press, 1986) explores the very particular tone of the prophets of exile – Jeremiah, Ezekiel and Isaiah 40-55. *Finally Comes the Poet: Daring Speech for Proclamation* (Fortress Press, 1989) is a challenge to preachers to re-discover the imaginative power of the biblical text. *Biblical Perspectives on Evangelism: Living in a Three-Storied Universe* (Abingdon Press, 1993) calls the church to re-connect with the transformative power of the gospel message. Written for an academic audience, but presented in an accessible and imaginative style, these relatively short books will be particularly helpful to those with some theological background who are looking to deepen their understanding of the application of Scripture to the contemporary world.

Graham Tomlin's *The Provocative Church* (SPCK, 2002, 2004) is a helpful and challenging consideration of the church's call to evangelism. Evangelism is, for Tomlin, not the task of a few select professionals but of the whole church, born of Christians living out a 'kingdom kind of life'. It is when the lives we lead cause those around us to ask 'what does this mean?' that true, biblical evangelism becomes possible. A book for all those wrestling with the role of the local church, and the central place of the individual believer, in the task of evangelism.

Movement for Change: Evangelical Perspectives on Social Transformation (Paternoster Press, 2004) is a collection of essays by some of the UK's leading thinkers on Christian social involvement. Edited by David Hilborn for the Evangelical Alliance's Commission on Unity and Truth, this book offers an excellent snapshot of recent evangelical thinking on this important area.

Spiritual Living in a Secular World (Monarch, 2002) by Ajith Fernando is a considered exploration of the relevance of Daniel for today's world. The national director of Youth for Christ Sri Lanka, and a renowned Bible teacher, Ajith Fernando knows well what it is to stand for biblical values in a hostile culture. Majoring on the godly character of Daniel, *Spiritual Living* will be of particular value to Christians living out their faith in the context of a secular workplace and community.

Conrad Gempf's *Jesus Asked: What He Wanted To Know* (Zondervan, 2003) is an unusual and intriguing exploration of the teaching style of Jesus. With some arresting insights and some surprising conclusions, Gempf seeks to re-discover the raw brilliance of Jesus the communicator. He does so by focusing not on the statements Jesus made, but on the questions he asked. A highly readable book that might well change the way you read the gospels – and the way you think about Jesus.

Dwelling in a Strange Land: Exile in the Bible and in the Church (SCM-Canterbury Press, 2003) by John Holdsworth was chosen in 2003 as a 'Lent book' by Rowan Williams, the archbishop of Canterbury. Academic in his theology but both poetic and pastoral in his style, John Holdsworth explores the impact that exile was to have on the theology of the people of Israel and asks what a 'theology of exile' might mean for the church today, particularly in a world darkened by the shadow of the events of 11 September 2001.

Brian McLaren's *The Church on the Other Side: Doing Ministry in the Postmodern Matrix* (Zondervan, 1998) is an updated and improved version of his earlier book *Reinventing Your Church*. A creative and fairly comprehensive exploration of what 'church' might look like in the new conditions of postmodern culture, this is a book full of insight, challenges and ideas. Written more for an American than a European context, *The Church on the Other Side* nonetheless has a huge amount to offer to believers navigating the 'journey into exile' of the early twenty-first century.

Day 4

Pressure:
Faith in the furnace

Outline of the Day:
Introduction: Pressure

Overview: Daniel 3 and 6

Teaching Block 1:   page 64
Pressure and persecution

Question Time

In The Zone

Teaching Block 2:   page 72
Pressure and paganism

Question Time

In The Zone

Teaching Block 3:   page 77
Pressure and prayer: forging a sustainable spirituality

Question Time

In The Zone

Conclusion: 'God meant it for good'

Books

Introduction: Pressure

"It's the power of the blues to sing about hope in the midst of despair which makes 'singing' such an authentic exercise for the marginalised." Joel Edwards

The story of Daniel in the lions' den is an established and abiding image in our culture. It has impacted the generations so deeply that Daniel is forever associated with this single and singular incident. Place it alongside the equally dramatic narrative of Shadrach, Meshach and Abednego in the 'fiery furnace' and you have the two stand-out stories of the book of Daniel. These are the incidents in which the theme of faith in exile is most graphically portrayed. Here the pressures of pagan Babylon become specific, focussed, life-threatening and intense – and God comes through. God is able, these stories resoundingly assert, to see his people through the pressures of adversity.

Overview: Daniel 3
The fire escape

Daniel chapter 3 concerns the three young Hebrews named as Daniel's companions in chapters 1 and 2. Promoted along with Daniel after his 'dream decoding' exploits, they have come to a place of prominence in Nebuchadnezzar's empire. But prominence brings its own complexities. There are rivalries and jealousies amongst the civil servants of different faiths, and the high profile given to the exiles draws stark attention to their distinction as Hebrews. They are pitted against the overwhelming power of Nebuchadnezzar himself, as he calls all his loyal servants to bow down to his image of gold.

"This Nebuchadnezzar is one whom God allowed to devastate and pillage the temple in Jerusalem, which David had enriched with 100,000 talents of gold; he is one who has been characterised in chapter 2 as the gold head of a multi-metalled statue. He now constructs an immense gold statue of his own. It was to be the most impressive statue that dispersion Jews would ever see, to be dedicated in the presence of as impressive a gathering of state dignitaries as they would ever witness, representing as many nations as they could ever envisage, at a ceremony heralded by as cosmopolitan an ensemble as they would ever hear." John Goldingay[104]

In refusing to worship this idolatrous statue, the three young Hebrews face the threat of death, which they meet with the remarkable words of the 'key verse' quoted above. Their faith is unshakeable – God can save them if he chooses, but if he chooses not to, he is still God. They will not bow. They are unburned by the flames. A fourth figure is seen mysteriously alongside them, and the emperor must acknowledge the superiority of their God. He honours Shadrach, Meshach and Abednego, congratulates them for having defied his very command (v 28), ratifies the public worship of their God and promotes them again: this time not just because they are associates of Daniel, but because they themselves have proved the power of God. Thus we are given one of Scripture's most memorable stories of faith under pressure – a story by which generations of God's followers have been uplifted.

"But when believers face some white-hot furnace they may be encouraged to be faithful to him, confident that their God is Lord of death and that he will demonstrate that he is. The power of paganism offers no ultimate threat. When situations are utterly hopeless, they can trust him to vindicate their commitment and his power by rescuing them one way or the other." John Goldingay[105]

Key verse:

If we are thrown into the blazing furnace, the God we serve is able to save us from it, and he will rescue us from your hand, O king. But even if he does not, we want you to know, O king, that we will not serve your gods or worship the image of gold you have set up.

Daniel 3:17–18

Day 4

The Good News Bible translation of Daniel 3:17 highlights an important aspect of the Hebrew faith.

"If the God whom we serve is able to save us from the blazing furnace and from your power, then he will. But even if he doesn't, Your Majesty may be sure that we will not worship your god..."

Other recent versions, including the New Revised Standard Version, agree with this translation, because it holds faithfully to an important theological truth about the Jewish faith: the exiles were committed to their God not primarily because of his *power*, but because of his *goodness*. It is because God is *good* that he can ultimately be trusted in all circumstances; and his goodness is not lost when circumstances seem to go against us.

Daniel 6: the dirty den

Daniel 6 is set over 60 years later, when Babylon has fallen to the Persians and Darius the Mede is its effective ruler. Daniel is once again given a prominent role in government, and once again the petty jealousies of his rivals are aroused. The story follows, in many ways, the pattern of the earlier adventure, as Daniel defies an order of the king, is denounced by his colleagues and must face death – this time in a pit of lions. Once again God's vindication is seen in preserving his servant *through* the trial.

"As Daniel's friends were not preserved from the furnace, so Daniel has not been preserved from the lion pit; as the divine aide entered the furnace to stand with Daniel's friends, so God has sent his aide into the pit to stand with Daniel; as Daniel's friends were preserved in the furnace, so is Daniel in the lion pit." John Goldingay[106]

In both stories it is the angel of the Lord who comes (3:25, 6:22), in both the servants of Yahweh emerge totally unharmed (3:27, 6:22) and in both the perhaps unwitting representatives of paganism are killed instead (3:22, 6:24). One subtle difference which makes this second story a complement to the first, rather than its duplication, is the reason for the sentence of death. It is not for refusing to worship idols that Daniel is singled out, but for refusing to *not worship* God.

"Daniel's obedience flowed from his realization that he would sin if he did not practise his own religion. In this way, it is the flip side of Daniel 3, where the three friends illustrated the realization that they would sin if they participated in the false religious practices of their idolatrous oppressors. The two chapters together thus encourage later readers to avoid false religion and to pursue legitimate religion, no matter what the cost." Tremper Longman[107]

Once again the response to the rescue is that the king acknowledges the superiority of Daniel's God, issuing a decree that the God of the Hebrews should be 'feared and reverenced' throughout the empire. God has been proved in the time of testing, and the result, yet again, is that Daniel prospers in the reign of this new king.

There is an intriguing twist to the second of these trial narratives in the portrayal of Darius, Babylon's new Persian ruler. Darius appears to genuinely favour Daniel, and doesn't want to persecute him at all, but he is trapped by his own pagan proclamations. He cannot rescind the decrees he himself has devised, so he must reluctantly put Daniel to the test.

"In other words, Darius, the most powerful human being in the world, has no power to save Daniel. But Daniel's faith is founded in a person who is more powerful than the king, God himself." Tremper Longman[108]

It is possible that the lions' den is not a means of execution at all, but a test of integrity – the Babylonian equivalent of a medieval ducking stool. If a person is suspected of disloyalty or deception, they can be locked in to this ultimate test. If 'the gods' preserve them, it is a mark of their integrity. It may be that Darius, far from wanting Daniel dead, is looking for a way out of his dilemma and resorts to this ultimate test in the desperate hope that Daniel *will* survive. This possibility is suggested by the wording of the story in several places, not least in the fact that it is the king himself who rushes to the lions' den after an allotted time has passed to find out if Daniel's God has preserved him.

Many Christian commentators have also been able to discern in this story the prefiguring of the resurrection of Jesus. Jesus faces the ultimate test – the 'lions' den' of death itself – as a stone is rolled across his tomb to mark him dead. But the stone is rolled away as the sun rises, and Jesus is found to be alive. He has faced, and passed, the ultimate test. He is the one who is God.

"For he is the living God and he endures forever; his kingdom will not be destroyed, his dominion will never end. He rescues and he saves; he performs signs and wonders in the heavens and on the earth." (Dan 6:26–27)

What can we learn?

These two dramatic stories serve together as a stark reminder that the God of the Bible is *with his people* in the pressures and trials they face. Two important aspects of this, common to both narratives, help to set the Bible's overall tone for the workings of faith under pressure.

- The first is that faith is not dependent on God's rescue. In both stories those facing death clearly believe that God is able to rescue them – *but this is not the basis of their faith*. They are loyal to God because he is God, and if they must die for their loyalty, so be it. Faith is rooted in who God is, not in what he does for those who serve him. This is of crucial importance to the Jews facing the horrors of exile in the sixth century and the persecutions of Antiochus Epiphanes in the second century, since in both cases God seemed to be allowing Israel to 'die'. God does not preserve his saints from their trials, but *in and through* their trials.

- The second is that the issue at stake in both stories is *worship*. It is for the freedom to worship Yahweh, and to resist the worship of idols, that the Hebrew heroes are standing. Worship is both the cause and the result of each of these trials, with both Nebuchadnezzar and Darius ultimately acknowledging God. This identifies worship as the central issue of exile. Daniel and his friends can bear the dislocation and deprivations of exile; they can cope with captivity, but they cannot – they will not – give up on worship. The Christians who have faced persecution in Communist and other totalitarian systems have predominantly done so for this same refusal to abandon worship. The freedom to worship God is not an optional gloss of faith that can easily be negotiated away – to the believer it is life itself.

The stories of the book of Daniel can be summed up in one sentence: *the worst that could happen has happened, and yet God reigns*. Nothing that has happened, will happen, can happen or might happen can *change the foundational reality of God's reign*. Wherever life takes you, whatever you face, God is with you – present, powerful and worthy of your worship.

Our exploration of 'faith in the furnace' will cover three important aspects:

- **Pressure and persecution** – how does Daniel's story help us find the strength to stand?

- **Pressure and paganism** – what if the danger we face is not the direct pain of persecution but the subtle seduction of our culture's substitute gods?

- **Pressure and prayer** – what does Daniel's life of prayer have to tell us about forging a sustainable spirituality in our pluralist, pagan environment?

Day 4

Teaching Block 1:
Pressure and persecution

> 1.1 Pressure clarifies the grounds of faith
> 1.2 Pressure turns faith into 'determined realism'
> 1.3 Pressure unlocks surprising springs of joy
> 1.4 Pressure calls the church to solidarity
> 1.5 Pressure bears fruit in love and mission

"If we're chucked into this blazing oven, the God we work for could pull us out alive. He'll rescue us from your cruelty, King. Even if he doesn't and we fry, you should still know, there'd be no regrets – no way are we bowing down to your gods or your overgrown gold Action Man." (Dan 3:17–18, The Street Bible)[109]

If we learn nothing else from these stories, we must surely learn that God is with his people in tough times. The witness of Scripture and of history is that it is very often in the worst of times – in the times of persecution, opposition, hardship and trial – that the greatest resources of faith are released. The pressures of adversity seem to serve, under God's hand, to open deeper wells of faith. For those of us who live in relatively undisturbed comfort, there are important lessons to be learned from God's people when they, like Daniel, are called to put their faith on the line.

1.1 Pressure clarifies the grounds of faith

"A faith that is based on good people thanking God because they've prospered has no answers at all in the face of an exile." John Holdsworth[110]

It is all too easy, in times of plenty, for our faith to be in God's blessings rather than in God himself. The gifts of God, rather than the one who has given them, become our focus. Adversity strips this away, leaving us naked before God's love, with only his presence to sustain us. Those who have lived through such times speak of the great discovery they have made: *that his presence is enough.*

"I have served in the ministry thirty years, almost thirty-one. I have come to understand that there are two kinds of faith. One says if and the other says though. One says: 'If everything goes well, if my life is prosperous, if I'm happy, if no one I love dies, if I'm successful, then I will believe in God and say my prayers and go to the church and give what I can afford.' The other says though: Though the cause of evil prosper, though I sweat in Gethsemane, though I must drink my cup at Calvary – nevertheless, precisely then, I will trust the Lord who made me. So Job cries: 'Though he slay me, yet will I trust Him.'" George Ross[111]

In some senses it can be said that it is *only* under pressure that true faith can emerge and grow. Faith is born of trust, and trust is at its strongest when it is all we have.

"Faith, then, is an assertion of trust, even when our circumstances point in a direction that seems to call into question God's goodness. Faith is a vision of what cannot be seen, a knowing of something that is beyond verifiable human knowledge. It is an assent to the inner witness of the Spirit that continues to keep a flame alive in us after all our efforts to snuff it out have failed." Tremper Longman[112]

1.2 Pressure turns faith into 'determined realism'

The assertion of the three young Hebrews that even if they are not rescued *God is still God* is a significant insight into faith under pressure. This is faith grounded not in fantasy and denial, but in determined realism. Dr Gordon Temple, who works with Torch Trust for the Blind and the 'Churches for All' programme, points out how meaningful this response can be to Christians facing long-term disability.

"How is it possible, we often ask ourselves, to come to God for healing in genuine faith, yet with the awareness that healing may not come? How do we manage the false expectations of well-meaning Christian friends whose own faith insists that we really ought to be healed by now? For those with long-term illness and disability, to ask God for healing is to put their faith, and the faith of others, on the line. The three friends who faced the furnace had faith – but they faced up to the possibility that the outcome of their faith might not be the outcome they had wished for or 'believed' for. Their strength came from the realization that the outcome was not going to change anything: either the standing of God in their eyes or the trust they were determined to place in Him. With this assurance they walked resolutely into the situation – and God showed his power. Disabled believers walk this tightrope time after time: trusting God for healing, and yet knowing, if no healing comes, that he is still God – and still worthy of their lifelong trust. And for those of us who have not (yet) experienced disability, let's not make the mistake of seeing disabled people as one-dimensional – defined only by their disability – with their only conceivable need being for healing. Instead, let's share their journey of faith as they, with all of us, face the multi-dimensional challenges of life for which an unshakable trust in God is the key to real victory." Gordon Temple[113]

In a culture in which faith is all too often confused with denial, self-deception and wishful thinking, this 'determined realism' is a welcome corrective. It refuses both the naivety that says that God *must* rescue me and the cynicism that says that he *can't*. It is open to God's supernatural intervention, but not insistent on it. It cries out for the display of God's power, but does not dictate the terms. This is a faith that holds out for the possibility of miracles, and creates space for miracles to come, but will not jump ship when miracles are slow in coming.

"In my travels overseas I have noticed a striking difference in the wording of prayers. Christians in affluent countries tend to pray; 'Lord, take this trial away from us!' I have heard prisoners, persecuted Christians, and some who live in very poor countries pray instead, 'Lord, give us the strength to bear this trial.'" Philip Yancey[114]

Anna Lee Stangl has visited, on behalf of Christian Solidarity Worldwide, many Christians unjustly imprisoned in Peru during the government's long struggle against the Shining Path guerrilla movement. Thousands of innocent citizens were incarcerated during these turbulent years, including many Christians, and many are still awaiting release. In her preface to *Trial by Fire*, the testimony of seven of these Christian prisoners, she notes this same determined realism in their faith.

"Choosing hope when logic tells you hope is useless can be a terrifying thing to do, as it leaves open the possibility for disappointment. I have to admit I often personally struggle to comprehend how some of these men and women cling to hope and to their faith even after ten years without, it seems, an answer from God."[115]

The pressures of adversity and loss can serve, sometimes, to remind us that *God is God* on his terms, not on ours. Even in his silence, God speaks love to us in volumes.

Day 4

1.3 Pressure unlocks surprising springs of joy

Perhaps the most beautiful gift that is given to the church by those who suffer is the 'great discovery' that in the worst of circumstances joy is found.

Anna Lee Stangl reports from her visits to the Christian prisoners of Peru.

"I have seen a light and a hope radiating from inside the dark, damp prison cells of Peru that I have rarely seen in a 'free' church. I have been the recipient of immense Christian generosity and hospitality from prisoners, who invited me to eat the precious food their impoverished family had brought for them on their weekly visit. I have heard the true sound of joy in the singing voices of prisoners who have no rational reason to be joyful. I have heard words of hope uttered in an impossible situation that convicted me of my own puny faith. Paradoxically, it is by going into these prisons that I am reminded what freedom really is."[117]

There are joys, it seems, that are only released through suffering; joys that we cannot know until our props and substitutes, our false comforters and fair-weather friends fall away.

1.4 Pressure calls the church to solidarity

But this does not mean that we should romanticise or sanitise the realities of suffering. The pain of persecution is real, and it is deep. On a global scale, with the perspective of history, it is the *normal Christian life*. Richard Wurmbrand's moving accounts of his years of sustained imprisonment, torture, inhumanity and deprivation in the prisons of communist Romania served for many years as a prophetic voice to the church in the West that the suffering of the body is real.

"Handcuffs with sharp nails on the insides were placed on our wrists. If we were totally still, they didn't cut us. But in the bitterly cold cells, when we shook with cold, our wrists would be torn by the nails. ... We Christians were sometimes forced to stand in wooden boxes only slightly larger than we were. This left no room to move. Dozens of sharp nails were driven into every side of the box, with their razor-sharp points sticking through the wood. While we stood perfectly still, it was all right. But we were forced to stand in these boxes for endless hours; when we became fatigued and swayed with tiredness, the nails would pierce our bodies. If we moved or twitched a muscle — there were the horrible nails. ... All biblical descriptions of hell and the pains of Dante's Inferno are nothing in comparison with the tortures in Communist prisons."[118]

Though European Communism is no longer the dark shadow it was Christian voices from many parts of the world continue to raise the same cry.

Christian Solidarity Worldwide reports:

- In Cuba Dr Oscar Biscet, a 42-year-old physician and human rights activist, was sentenced to 25 years imprisonment and lives in a punishment cell with no window or light; Juan Carlos Gonzales Leiva, a blind Christian human rights lawyer, has been been in prison for two years without trial.

- In 2004 in Nigeria, 48 people were murdered in an attack at a church service and on 11 May violence in Kano left at least 600 people dead when 10,000 protesting Muslims attacked Christian targets.

- In Colombia more than 40 church leaders were assassinated by armed groups in 2003.

The question is, do those parts of the body not abused *hear*?

"When I was beaten on the bottom of my feet, my tongue cried. Why did my tongue cry? It was not beaten. It cried because the tongue and feet are both part of the same body. And you free Christians are part of the same Body of Christ that is now beaten in prisons, [and] restricted nations, that even now gives martyrs for Christ. Can you not feel our pain?"[119]

Very often it is the support offered by the church worldwide that enables Christians suffering appalling persecution to survive.

Rev Rinaldy Damanik, an Indonesian church leader jailed for three years, writes:
"Thank you to everyone who has prayed for me. I really felt the power of your prayers in prison and they strengthened my faith. I also want to thank all of those who wrote to me. They brought light into my life."

Ricardo Esquivia Ballestas, a Colombian church leader and human rights activist, writes:
"Your expressions of solidarity are signs of life, hope and freedom."

1.5 Pressure bears fruit in love and mission

Lastly, it is also clear from Scripture and from history that pressure on God's people can serve to wring from them a response not of hatred but of love. Open opposition, very often, can produce a deeper love reaction than benign tolerance.

- This is the witness of Nelson Mandela, who says it was imprisonment that wrought in him the capacity to place mercy alongside justice.

"It was during those long and lonely years that my hunger for the freedom of my own people became a hunger for the freedom of all people, white and black. I knew as well as I know anything that the oppressor must be liberated just as surely as the oppressed."[120]

- It is the witness of Tertullian, chronicler of the sufferings of the early church.

"Your cruelty [against us] does not profit you, however exquisite. Instead, it tempts people to our sect. As often as you do us down, the more we grow in number. ... The very obstinacy you criticise teaches for us. For who on seeing it is not excited to enquire what lies behind it? Who, having enquired, does not embrace our faith?"[121]

- It is the witness of Martin Luther King, who understood that it is in discovering the *strength to love* that the ultimate justice is found.

"To our most bitter opponents we say: 'We shall match your capacity to inflict suffering by our capacity to endure suffering. We shall meet your physical force with soul force. ... Throw us into jail, and we shall still love you. Send your hooded perpetrators of violence into our community at the midnight hour and beat us and leave us half dead and we shall still love you. But be ye assured that we will wear you down by our capacity to suffer. One day we shall win freedom, but not only for ourselves. We shall so appeal to your heart and conscience that we shall win you in the process, and our victory will be a double victory.'"[122]

In our understanding and practice of our faith, it is vital that we hear these many voices. Suffering, by this reading – when the pressures of opposition and adversity break into our lives and oppress us – has been God's means, since the cross itself, of bringing his love into the world. Richard Wurmbrand uses one final, compelling image from Daniel 3 to summarise his own experience of this truth.

"As in the book of Daniel when the three young men who were put in the furnace did not smell like the fire upon being delivered from it, so the Christians who have been in Communist prisons don't smell like bitterness against the Communists. A flower, if you bruise it under your feet, rewards you by giving you its perfume. Likewise Christians tortured by the Communists, reward their torturers by love."[124]

Pressure

Day 4

In The Zone

If 'pressure as persecution' can unlock deeper wells of faith, of joy and of love, this will have implications for the ways we react and respond to negative circumstances. In the context of the Zone you are exploring, consider the impact that this might have on the pressures you face.

- *Faith and a Changing World*
  In our own culture and context, is direct opposition to the Christian faith likely to increase or decrease in the years ahead? What are the implications for our churches, and for the practice of our faith?

- *Faith and the Developing World*
  What lessons are there for us to learn from our brothers and sisters in God's global family for whom the *normal* Christian life is a life of poverty and persecution? For those of us still living in our 'first choice' world, what does the expression of solidarity imply?

- *Faith and Devotional Life*
  How does the suggestion that pressure 'opens deeper wells' impact the ways we pray? What are the implications of recognising the pressures and adversities we face as *God's most valued teachers* as we seek a deeper devotional experience?

- *Faith and Everyday Life*
  What are the areas in your experience in which pressure has served to open deeper wells of faith? How might this change the way you view the negative circumstances you encounter day by day?

- *Faith and Family Life*
  Is it possible for the pressures families face – in strained relationships, financial hardships and the struggles of parenting – to become a shared resource in the search for a deeper faith? In teaching and discipling our children, what is the impact of their observation of the way their parents and elders respond to pressure?

- *Faith and Involvement*
  What are the areas in public life in which opposition and adversity can lead to a deeper expression of the Christian faith? Are there times when the way Christians respond to pressure can be a silent commendation of their faith?

- *Faith and Working Life*
  What are the situations in the workplace in which Christians might face the pressures of opposition and adversity? How can these become 'openings' for a deeper faith and stronger witness?

Question Time

It is very often the pressures we face that bring out in us the very fruits of faith, joy and love that God is growing. In your own experience and that of those close to you:

- Are there times when you have known or observed adversity and suffering, and seen from it the fruits described above?

- Does the description of faith as 'determined realism' resonate with your experience of prayer, and of the life of the church?

- If the sufferings of the body of Christ call us to stand as one and to weep with those who weep, what might the implications be for our prayers and for the worship lives of our churches?

Voices in Exile:
Release International – Nageena's story

Her mother was the only one to hear her story. The seven-year-old whispered it once, and since then has hardly talked at all.

She was returning from a friend's house at 11.30 am, when someone called out. As she turned, four men from her village ran towards her. Nageena ran too, tripping on her scarf, stumbling on the unmade road. She is not sure why she ran – because they were running, because they had never spoken to her, because the only man she had ever talked to was her father. But the four men were faster, cornering her, catching her.

She could remember being pushed through a wooden door into a dark room. She screamed, but could not describe what happened next.

Villagers heard her crying and a crowd gathered outside the cowshed. Ghulam Masih saw the commotion, ran over and pulled open the door. Inside he saw Alla, Ditta, Rashid and Gavic, the sons of his neighbour standing over his daughter, her clothes tangled with straw, her legs covered with blood. As he scooped Nageena into his arms, the four men backed away and ran across a field.

Nageena's father and mother carried their daughter to the police station, filed a criminal complaint and were put on a bus to Shekhupura Hospital, in Pakistan's Punjab Province. It was 10.30 pm by the time they arrived. The duty doctor was about to go home. However his medical report concluded that Nageena's internal injuries were so severe that she would never be able to have children.

Over the next two weeks, as Nageena hid under her hospital blanket, the Sharqpur police arrested the four men, after dozens of villagers came forward with their names.

It would be another six weeks before Nageena would speak again to her mother, and when she did it was to ask why the four rapists were back in the village.

Mushtaq Ahmed, an inspector of police, had freed them and closed the case. He said he could find no evidence and told Nageena's family to forget the matter. But Ghulam continued to demand justice and refused gifts of a new home, money, sweets and clothes from the men who had raped his daughter.

Nineteen months later, the family thought their determination had paid off. They received a letter from a new government department, the Human Rights Ministry of Pakistan, which said it had reviewed the criminal file and had decided to award Nageena £200 compensation.

Two weeks later, Ghulam Masih was back at Sharqpur Police Station. This time he was lying half naked with his face in the dirt, iron chains around his wrists and ankles. Inspector Mushtaq Ahmed, who had supervised the rape case, was now ordering his officers to beat Ghulam in order to extricate a confession. Ghulam was accused of the killing of an old woman and his accusers were his daughter's rapists.

Why had the word of four men who were accused of the rape of a child been acted upon without investigation, while the report of Nageena's assault gathered dust in the inspector's office?

'The prisoner is a Christian,' Inspector Mushtaq said, 'and the men who are accused of raping his daughter are good Muslims. I have no reason to disbelieve them, as they are good Muslims. My first duty is to Islam. The courts will take a similar view and Ghulam Masih will be hanged. You'll see.'

After 14 days of internment a Lahore High Court bailiff rushed to the prison, and forced an order into the police inspector's hands. Ghulam was freed but the charge against him still remains. Now for security reasons he has to live in hiding and Nageena has found safety in a Christian sanctuary.

The story of Nageena and Ghulam seems difficult to believe: a little girl, mute from assault; a father facing a death sentence for pursuing justice.

Day 4

Nageena was raped because she was a Christian. In the eyes of her attackers her religion made her worthless, vulnerable and unlikely to be believed. Her father is facing a death sentence because he dared to challenge a judicial system in which the word of a Muslim is officially worth more than that of a Christian.

When I met Nageena, she was part of a worship group at a seminar to help women see their value in God. At 12 years of age, the five years since this incident have brought a measure of healing, although there is still a long way to go.

As I watched her caught up in worship, I marvelled at God's goodness in restoring her to the extent that she can now be involved in leading others into the healing presence of God.

Voices in Exile:
Dan Bauman – Imprisoned in Persia

(Dan Bauman is an 'ordinary American' who was arrested in Iran in 1997, while travelling with YWAM. Interrogated as a US spy, he was imprisoned on false charges of espionage and spent ten weeks in the notorious Evin high-security prison in Tehran. Locked 24 hours a day in his cell, with no indication of how or when he might be released, he faced horrific fears. Day fourteen of his ordeal was his lowest point, when he was so tormented by panic that he tried to take his own life. He pulled back at the last moment.)

I sat stunned at how close I had come to throwing my life away. Guilt and remorse washed over me in waves, and I began to cry out to God. "Please forgive me, God. I give myself back to you," I prayed. "The only place I am safe is in your presence. I will stay in prison the rest of my life if that is where you want me. But I promise, no matter what happens, I will never try to kill myself again. I know it's not the way you have for me to get out of this place. I will walk the path you have made for me and try not to make my own way. Amen."

Following the suicide attempt, I felt closeness with God that I had not experienced in prison up until this time. I had a new joy and certainty in my heart. And I sensed a new expectation inside that I couldn't explain. I had a deep conviction that something significant was going to happen the next day. Somehow I knew God was going to say something important to me then.

By 7 a.m. the next day, I was so excited I could barely stand it. However, I made myself follow my usual morning routine. I read two psalms at seven and waited until about eight before I picked up my Bible again. Before I began reading, I prayed. "God, I know you are here with me, and I sense you have something special to say this morning. Please guide me now." I opened my eyes, sure God was about to speak to me.

I randomly opened my Bible and, looking down, saw it was opened at the Old Testament book of Daniel, chapter ten. My eyes fell on verses twelve and thirteen. I read them expectantly. "Then he continued, 'Do not be afraid, Daniel. Since the first day that you set your mind to gain understanding and to humble yourself before your God, you words were heard, and I have come in response to them. But the prince of the Persian kingdom resisted me twenty-one days. Then Michael, one of the chief princes, came to help me, because I was detained there with the king of Persia.'"

I scooted back and leaned against the wall, hardly able to take in what I had just read. I had never before felt such a powerful sense that God was speaking to me through Scripture as I felt at that moment. I read the passage again. *"Do not be afraid, Daniel."* Okay, I told myself, I am not to be afraid any more. *"Since the first day that you set your mind to gain understanding and to humble yourself before your God, your words were heard, and I have come in response to them."* God had been with me the whole time, watching over me. *"But the prince of the Persian kingdom resisted me twenty-one days."* Wow! I got goose bumps as I re-read those words. It had been exactly twenty-one days since my passport had been taken from me at the border.

Now I was in prison, and not just any prison, but a high-security prison in the heart of the Persian kingdom.

I read on and became even more excited when I got to verse nineteen. "'*Do not be afraid, O man highly esteemed,' he said. 'Peace! Be strong now; be strong.'*"

The word *peace* resonated within me. For the first time since I had been arrested, I knew everything was going to work out. A voice inside said, "You will get out in my way, and in my time." I also knew beyond a shadow of doubt that God had allowed me to be put in prison for a purpose. I was in his hands. Even though I couldn't see the bigger picture, he could, and I intended to trust him totally from that moment on.

Throughout the rest of the day, I reread that passage many times, and with each reading, hope welled within me. I was exactly where God wanted me to be. I might feel as though I were in the pit of hell, but I was not there by accident. I was there because God had a definite plan for me to be there, whether I understood it or not.[125]

Voices in Exile:
Ian Coffey – Picturing peace

A visitor to an art gallery found that two exhibits shared the same title. The paintings were entitled 'Peace' but were totally different. The first was a rural landscape in which the artist had captured a perfect summer's day. The picture oozed tranquility and invitingly beckoned the viewer to feel the warm sun and hear the gentle sounds of nature.

The second was a seascape with dark clouds and lashing rain. The picture showed a cliff-face standing proud against an angry sea. Everywhere was violent movement but in the cleft of a rock the artist had painted a bird in its nest. In the middle of a raging storm, the bird was resting in complete safety.

Those two interpretations of peace offer us a parable in troubled times. For some, peace is like a tranquil summer's day when nothing appears to disturb the picture. It is all about cloudless skies and endless sunshine. Thank God, such times do come.

But in reality, life is not always like that. Whichever scale we use to measure – global or personal, macro or micro – life produces storms from time to time. Interestingly, the second picture, of the bird resting in the middle of a howling gale, is closer to the Bible's teaching about God's gift of peace. Peace is not so much the absence of trouble but the relaxation of heart and mind that comes in the midst of trouble.

As one writer of a previous generation has expressed it:

"If God be our God, he will give us peace in trouble. When there is a storm without, he will make peace within. The world can create trouble in peace, but God can create peace in trouble."

Peace *with* God is a gift that all can enjoy because of Jesus. On the basis of this new relationship we can experience the peace *of* God in every circumstance that life throws up.[126]

Day 4

Teaching Block 2:
Pressure and paganism

> 2.1 Permissive pluralism can be as strong a foe as paganism
> 2.2 All idolatry is to be resisted
> 2.3 'God-substitutes' are idols just as 'gods' are
> 2.4 Resistance calls for 'inner non-compliance'
> 2.5 Resistance is not only for the young!

It is important to acknowledge, in the life of Daniel, that God enabled his faithful servant to resist not only the intense pressures of persecution, when these arose, but also the ongoing pressures of assimilation. Daniel and his friends found the strength to fight both the direct threats of lions' den and furnace *and* the more subtle seductions of a powerful and pervasive pagan culture. The structure of the narrative suggests a link between these two, with the self-imposed 'food fast' of chapter 1 given a prominent place in the story because it sets the tone for all that is to follow. Newly arrived in Babylon the young Hebrews, with Daniel taking the initiative to lead them, are:

- Able to discern the idolatrous roots of the culture in which they find themselves. Though ready and willing to engage with their new context, they know they will be called upon to 'draw the line' at worship. Being captive to a more powerful culture is something over which they have no choice: but the worship of their hearts is theirs to give or to withhold, and the line of non-co-operation they draw is drawn on the issue of idolatrous worship.

- Able to pursue a path of non-conformity to the dominant values of Babylon, where these touch on matters of personal holiness and integrity. Daniel and his friends do not go looking for trouble. They do not seem to see the 'reform' of Babylonian culture as their priority, no matter how strongly we might want to 'read this in' to the text. But they do pursue a life of quiet non-conformity, and are ready and willing to make a public stand whenever their non-cooperation is exposed. The goal of their non-conformity is that they must not 'defile themselves' in Babylon (Dan 1:8). According to a framework of personal holiness to which we are not privy, they establish what the parameters of their non-conformity will be.

It is because they have been able to discern Babylon's idolatrous roots, and because they are committed, where God requires it, to non-conformity that the exiles are able, when pressure comes, to stand. This answers the question that is most puzzling of all in the story of Daniel, how he knew so clearly when to accept compromise and when not to. The answer suggested by the narrative is that Daniel made two high-level personal commitments in adapting to a life in exile.

- His worship would be reserved for God alone. He would make a stand, therefore, whenever an idolatrous act of worship was required of him.

- He would pursue a life of non-conformity wherever his personal holiness and integrity were at stake.

From the efforts of the exiles to 'live for God' in Babylon, and reserve their worship only for Yahweh, we can draw four key principles for our own exilic journey.

2.1 Permissive pluralism can be as strong a foe as paganism

It is all too easy to assume that the pressure on Daniel to give in to the worship of idols and abandon the worship of Yahweh is qualitatively different to the pressures we face today. But sixth century Babylon was remarkably akin to today's postmodern, pluralist culture. Like Athens in the New Testament period (Acts 17) and the world's major cities today, Babylon offered all kinds of worship to all kinds of gods.

"In Nebuchadnezzar's Babylon, for example, the eight city gates were named after different gods. Even more striking is the fact that temples dedicated to Adad, Shamash, Ninurta, Ishtar and numerous other deities existed simultaneously in the city." Daniel Block[127]

Daniel was not under pressure to worship a particular pagan god so much as to go along with the *laissez-faire* pluralism that allowed for any and all gods. He could pray to Yahweh if he wished, just so long as he did not make his worship *exclusive*. To resist this pressure, insisting on his God's claim to exclusive worship, was to live in faithfulness to the long-standing Old Testament rejection of all idolatry.

For Daniel, as for us, the issue was not only the freedom to worship Yahweh; it was the freedom to worship Yahweh *as the only God*. A faith in which our God is one god amongst many is unlikely to be challenged in a pluralist, tolerant culture, but a faith in which our God demands exclusive worship will lead us unavoidably to non-compliance.

2.2 All idolatry is to be resisted

Resisting idolatry was one of the foundational commitments of the Hebrew faith. This is why it is around issues of *worship*, rather than politics, economics or social justice, that Daniel and his friends choose most often to resist. Whatever else God asks of his people, he asks that they have 'no other gods'.

"Idolatrous practices are treated as spiritual harlotry (Jdg 2:17, 8:27, 8:33), an abomination (Deut 32:15), detestable (Deut 29:16), foolishness (Isa 40:18–20; 41:6–7; 44:9–20; 46:1–2; Jer 10:1–10; Psa 115:1–8), and utterly disgusting (Ezek 8:10). According to the orthodox Yahwist, the God of Israel would brook no rivals. In this respect the Hebrew view of Israel's relationship to its patron deity differed fundamentally from the perceptions of all the other nations around." Daniel Block[128]

Worship that honours God as one amongst many is simply not enough. Yahweh makes exclusive and comprehensive claims, and these are taken up and reinforced in Jesus. The God of the Bible is not simply *my* God but *the one true God*, and this alone is enough to bring the faithful believer into social conflict. God asks us to love and worship him above any and every rival – and every affection that lays claim to our heart has the potential to become an idol to us.

2.3 'God substitutes' are idols just as 'gods' are

Following the analysis of Christian philosopher Herman Dooyeweerd, Pete Lowman suggests that the history of our culture can be understood as a commitment to a succession of idols – each of which has, in turn, failed us.

"We can re-express it like this: in each era since we turned away from the Bible's God, our culture has been shaped by one or more 'god-substitutes'. These aren't gods that we actually 'worship', but they're the next thing to it. They're the things that 'matter most' to us, the principles that dominate our lives, determining our sense of what's important and

the sources we look to for truth and meaning, for the understanding of right and wrong. Our culture's story is, among other things, the history of successive 'god-substitutes', and of how well they 'reign' as our gods. One after another they hold this role, until their inadequacies become obvious; when we lose faith in them, they are replaced by a different 'god', and the story begins again." Pete Lowman[129]

Idolatry in this analysis is not just the worship of gods of wood and stone, but also the worship of 'god substitutes' – the ideas and values that we trust to guide our lives and culture.

"At first it is difficult for us as Christians living at the turn of the millennium to identify with the challenge facing the Jewish people on the plain of Dura. But we have suggested that the issue transcends the worship of a particular statue and concerns instead the constant threat to dilute the worship of the true God by elevating anything or anyone else to a comparable place of importance in our life. As John Calvin has provocatively charged, the human mind is a 'factory of idols'. We are constantly, even as Christians, in a struggle with this temptation." Tremper Longman[130]

Perhaps we would find resistance easier if we *were* asked to bow down to a 90-foot gold statue. The harder task is to know when it is that the dominant commitments of our culture – to materialism or power; to militarism or industry; to a particular model of family or community; even to ways of being church – have become idolatrous. But this is the task to which, as exiles, we are called.

2.4 Resistance calls for 'inner non-compliance'

Though the 'high-points' of resistance in chapters 3 and 6 relate quite clearly to issues of public worship and private prayer, the book of Daniel is relatively silent as to what the decisive issues of idolatry were at other times. Daniel's choice in chapter 1 to accept the imposition of a name – honouring a pagan God – but to refuse the king's food is foundational to the book. It demonstrates that he was thinking through what the issues might be, but it does not let us in on the detail of his thinking. Throughout his life, Daniel clearly knew when to conform and when not to, but the book is silent on the exact basis of his choices. Rather, we are left with a dual principle.

• Issues of holiness and personal integrity will be different in different times and places.

• Each of us is called, in our own culture and context, to discern just where the lines are drawn.

The pressure to conform will present itself in different ways in different lives, reflecting in different particularities the 'tone and textures' of a culture's given idols.

"The pressure to be faithful comes in many different ways. For many Christians in active and influential places it may well be the power of seduction. At one stage Daniel's pressure to conform was simply a decision not to eat a meal. For us it may be the decision to refuse a promotion, terminate a friendship or turn down a TV appearance." Joel Edwards[131]

The narrative does not, in its silence, authorise us to ignore the call to non-compliance, but calls us, rather, to the hard work of discerning just what the decisive issues are in each of our lives. Walter Brueggemann suggests that Daniel's thought-through non-conformity can serve as a dynamic model in the pressures of seduction we face in our own day.

"Daniel prevailed over exile, and in the process he maintained freedom in his faith. He did not conform. He did not attempt to gain or enhance his worth by conforming, nor to save his life by keeping it. Sustained by faith, Daniel is his own man as he is God's man, and he does not conform. The text is not, I submit, remote from our own situation in which pressures in church and in society to conform are great. We imagine our worth comes in conforming, in unquestioning obedience, in responding quickly to every opinion poll of

preference. The conforming happens subtly, not frontally. We join the dominant ideology with innocence and without noticing. In the congregation are those who do not notice their conformity and thus are incapable of imagining any alternative. We may notice how 'the others' have conformed; we are not so skilful in noticing how we ourselves have joined the version of ideology most compatible with our social location and interest." Walter Brueggemann[132]

Daniel's response is not only to refuse the route of dull conformity, but to mark out an alternative route. He pursues an inner non-compliance, finding creative ways to express his Hebrew identity, and he is ready to pay the price when those ways are resisted by Babylon's powers.

"The text invites people like us, at the door of capitulation, to think about an alternative. The proffered alternative is this: Remember who you are by remembering whose you are. Be your own person even in the face of the empire, of the dominant ideology, of the great power of death. Be your own person by being in the company of the great God who works in, with, and through the training programme of the empire for the sake of God's own people. Be your own person, because God has not succumbed to the weight of the empire." Walter Brueggemann[133]

It is left to each of us to work out, alone and in community, what the pressure to conform might mean in our particular life setting, and how we might show in the act of remembering who we are that we have remembered whose we are.

2.5 Resistance is not only for the young!

One of the remarkable aspects of the book of Daniel is that it shows its hero having the same discernment, courage and conviction at the end of his life and career as at the beginning. Daniel does not only resist idols when he has the strength and energy of youth on his side; he continues to do so well into his retirement years.

There is both an encouragement and a challenge here for those in later life: an encouragement that God has purposes yet to be fulfilled in every life; but a challenge, too, that the call to resist idolatry, to stay true to faith, to be a voice for integrity and worship in our culture remains strong to the very end of our days.

This is an aspect of Daniel's life that has much to say to us in the contemporary world, according to Doug Barnett.

"Dr. William Dorland, Chicago, researched the lives of hundreds of important men and discovered that 'sixty was the average age at which four hundred of the famous men of history did their best work.'

Many Bible notables were rich in years:

Noah was building an ark when most people of his age are on Zimmer instruction.

Abraham and Sarah produced children in extremely advanced years. Moses, 80, was leading the people out of the bondage of slavery in Egypt. Caleb, 85, claimed his promised inheritance, after waiting 45 years for it, and was immediately plunged into a punch up with his enemies. Joshua, around 70, led the people into Canaan and conflict. Daniel, at 70, was still serving and standing firm for God in difficult circumstances. Anna, 85, exercised a ministry of prayer in the Temple. Paul, 70, declared, 'I can do everything through him who gives me strength' in Philippians 4 v 13. John, at 90, composed the book of Revelation.

Their testimony is a clear and simple one – all can serve regardless of age. That service may be different from what has been done before but it need not be less effective. When a person comes to retirement for whatever reason and at whatever age, their professional experience and expertise in computing, child care, accountancy, secretarial work, administration, catering, nursing, car mechanics, carpentry and building can be of immense value to Christian and charitable organisations. Ask your church minister, pastor, elders, leaders what ministry you can have in the church.

Don't regret growing older, it is a privilege that is denied to many people. Rejoice in it

Day 4

and all the potential it holds for you. There are an endless number of things that can be done and learned. Never lose your sense of wonder and delight in the possibilities of each day. You can do things in your mature years that couldn't be done when you were younger.

What you lack in physical energy you can make up for with spiritual enthusiasm and life commitment. Dare to be a Daniel and stay with the programme until you get promoted to 'higher service.'"[134]

Question Time

This teaching block has suggested that seduction can be as powerful a force as persecution, drawing us in to the worship of idols. In your own experience of faith in our changing culture:

- What evidence do you see that Christians and their churches have been 'seduced' into the culture's dominant ideas?

- Is it possible to clearly recognise the idols or 'god substitutes' that are honoured in our culture?

- How might a call to 'inner non-compliance' be expressed in regard to the particular god substitutes we have identified?

In The Zone

What are the subtle seductions evident in the Zone you are exploring? What shape might inner non-compliance take in that area?

- *Faith and a Changing World*
  What god substitutes are fading from our culture as it changes, and what new god substitutes might be emerging? How might this impact the stand that the church is called to take?

- *Faith and the Developing World*
  How does the issue of god substitutes affect the way we define development and work with believers in other cultures? Are there principles in the area of resisting idolatry that are applicable to every culture and context?

- *Faith and Devotional Life*
  How does God's exclusive claim to the worship of our hearts impact our understanding of prayer and the devotional life? Are there things we can do in prayer to identify and root out the idolatrous commitments in our lives?

- *Faith and Everyday Life*
  What are the ways in which the world around us seduces us to follow substitutes for God? What kind of strategies do we need to resist this subtle seduction and live a life of inner non-compliance?

- *Faith and Family Life*
  What are the god substitutes that put pressure on family life, and how can we resist them? Are there ways in which the family or household can model inner non-compliance?

- *Faith and Involvement*
  Is there a place in public life for the Christian to discern and denounce the culture's dominant god substitutes? What are the implications of inner non-compliance for those giving time and energy to public service?

- *Faith and Working Life*
  Do the dominant god substitutes of a given organisation or employer make their presence felt in the workplace? How can Christians both resist and reform – helping others to identify and abandon the worship of idols?

Teaching Block 3:
Pressure and prayer: forging a sustainable spirituality

3.1 The priority of prayer: first things first
3.2 The depths of prayer: the freedom of discipline
3.3 The habit of prayer: the fabric of life
3.4 The outcome of prayer: the favour of God

The third important lesson of these narratives of rescue – particularly Daniel's story in chapter 6 – is that there is a significant relationship between pressure and prayer. The picture given of Daniel praying at his open window, facing his lost home in Jerusalem, is of

- a man who has made prayer a priority in his life. Daniel was doubtless called upon in the course of his work to negotiate and even compromise on many issues. But on this issue he was firm, he would not give up the right to pray.

- a man who looks to a life of prayer for strength and for sustenance through difficult times. By looking towards Jerusalem, Daniel is associating prayer with his most urgent need in exile – but also with the deepest longings of his own heart. Prayer is not a technical recitation of a list of requests – it is actually an intimate longing for the heart's true home.

- a man who holds to prayer as a daily discipline, a pattern at the very heart of the daily

routine. Daniel prays three times a day and he continues to pray 'just as he had done before'(6:10): The implication is of a long-standing habit. Prayer was central to the very fabric of Daniel's life in Babylon.

- a man who rejoices to record and celebrate the God who answers prayer. Because he prays, Daniel has no hesitation in acknowledging God's answer. There is no ambiguity for Daniel in explaining how good outcomes have arrived – they are the direct actions of a God who delights to answer his servant's prayers.

"The stories of Daniel make clear that one reason for this [his extraordinary spirit] was his intimacy with God, expressed and maintained by prayer. It was his regular habit of prayer that gave him the strength to ignore the king's new law. To have changed that habit, giving the appearance of fearing the king more than God, would have affected his intimacy with God, whom he would have felt he had betrayed in some measure." Ernest Lucas[135]

3.1 The priority of prayer:
first things first

In the history of the Christian church, there are almost as many ways of praying as there are Christians to pray. Means and methods of prayer vary from culture to culture and from century to century. But there is a pattern that emerges from the study of prayer that cannot be denied: It is those who make prayer a priority who most find themselves embraced by an answering God. As we pray, our knowledge of God deepens; we learn to recognise his voice and to discern his will; we begin to see our own circumstances

from his perspective. Whatever style and system we adopt in prayer, there is a rule so basic our faith would not exist without it – *those who make prayer their personal priority will come to know God more fully than those who pray begrudgingly, fulfilling a reluctant duty.*

"Authentic Christianity is not learning a set of doctrines and then stepping into cadence with people all marching the same way. It is not simply humanitarian service to the less

Day 4

fortunate. It is a walk, a supernatural walk with a living, dynamic, communicating God. Thus the heart and soul of the Christian life is learning to hear God's voice and developing the courage to do what he tells us to do." Bill Hybels[136]

Prayer will be there for us as a response and a resource in times of war if we have made prayer a priority and a practice in times of peace.

3.2 The depths of prayer:
the freedom of discipline

"The soul must long for God in order to be set aflame by God's love; but if the soul cannot yet feel this longing, then it must long for the longing. To long for the longing is also from God." Meister Eckhart[137]

Prayer is, in the words of Richard Foster, the heart's true home.[138] It is in prayer that the deepest longing of our souls is satisfied; that *'who we truly are'* is released. For centuries contemplatives have taught us that prayer is more than berating God with our needs: it is romance, fulfilment, warfare, joy, release. Far from binding us in dull routines of drudgery, the deeper disciplines of prayer free us for a life more full than we could ever, without prayer, aspire to.

"There is an awakening amongst many believers today who are no longer satisfied with the hustle and bustle generally known as the Christian life. Call it the deeper life, the contemplative life, or whatever you will. By any name this quality of Christian life is conceived in divine intimacy and born in quiet moments spent between two lovers. Many Christians who are dissatisfied with the emptiness of the noise are hearing his gentle call to something deeper, richer." Steve McVey[139]

Perhaps the greatest fruit of a deeper knowledge of God is that we find our fears diminishing. On seventy-nine occasions Scripture records the command 'fear not'[140] and one of the outcomes in our lives of deeper prayer is that when trouble arises we are less prone to panic. Our response to pressure is no longer distorted by fear. The opposite of fear, which is not courage but *trust*, becomes our foundation.

The outworking of this depth and confidence is seen in the patterns and passions of a later prayer, recorded in Daniel 9:4–19. This intercessory prayer projects its trust in God on to the national and international scene. The book of Daniel has resources for prayer far beyond the personal and pietistic: it promotes a history-changing view of prayer's power.

We will have the strength and security, the depth and discipline to face life's pressures when at the centre of our being we have learned to draw on the resources of God's presence. When we know intimacy with God in the inner sanctuary of the soul, we will know confidence with God in the outer battles of our Babylon.

3.3 The habit of prayer:
the fabric of life

It has been proven many times over in the history of the church, in many different traditions, that the most effective 'level' of spirituality is when prayer and worship are woven into the activities of every day, so that life is immersed in prayer. This is the mark of the Jewish life; a life that Daniel's 'three times a day' routine would surely have been an effort to reproduce in the absence of temple, priest or public worship. Influential spiritualities such as Brother Lawrence's

Practising the Presence of God and Jean-Pierre de Caussade's *The Sacrament of the Present Moment*, and others, have helped thousands of Christians to experience and enjoy God's presence in the everyday stuff of ordinary life.

"True spirituality does not make us angels but fully human – like Jesus." R. Paul Stevens[141]

An ancient prayer in the Celtic tradition

includes a 'liturgy' for the washing of the face in which three palmfuls of water are thrown in the name of the Trinity.

> *"The palmful of the God of Life,*
> *The palmful of the Christ of Love,*
> *The palmful of the Spirit of Peace,*
> *Triune of Grace."*[142]

Kenda Creasy Dean, in her book *The Godbearing Life: The Art of Soul Tending for Youth Ministry*, describes a moving contemporary application of this same prayer.

"A mother of two daughters remembers when, as a teenager she anguished over the acne on her face. One day she was so depressed she felt unable to leave the house. Her father led her to the bathroom and asked if he could teach her a new way to wash. He leaned over the sink and splashed water over his face, telling her,

> *'On the first splash, say, "In the name of the Father"; on the second, "In the name of the Son"; and on the third, "In the name of the Holy Spirit". Then look up into the mirror and remember that you are a child of God, full of grace and beauty.'*

Today this woman re-enacts those words at her daughters' bath time, making every bath a baptismal act, a reminder that they are made in God's image."[143]

Acne may not be your particular problem, and sacred face-washing may not be your chosen path, but what will it take for you to weave prayer, as Daniel did, into the very fabric of your daily life?

We will be more able to avail ourselves of the presence and power of God in extraordinary moments, when pressures and perversities, our own needs and the needs of others weigh down upon us, if we have learned to know and celebrate God's presence in the ordinary. We will know God's presence in the hard days and the heavy days because we have learned to know God's presence in the everyday.

3.3 The outcome of prayer:
the favour of God

Why does God answer prayer? Is it because of our eloquence, and the repetitive passion with which we petition him? No – it is because of his great kindness and mercy. Even the most inarticulate, unpolished and desperate of prayers can release God's favour. Roy Lawrence tells the story of a hospital chaplain who was asked to visit a particularly distraught patient. This man, in the terminal stages of cancer, was wracked with guilt because he had spent the previous night venting his anger at God. Raging and swearing, he had told the Eternal just what he thought of him – and in the morning he felt dreadful.

"He imagined that his chance of eternal life had now been lost forever, and that God would never forgive one who had so cursed and abused him.

The chaplain asked this patient, 'What do you think is the opposite of love?'

The man replied, 'Hate.'

Very wisely, the chaplain replied, 'No, the opposite of love is indifference. You have not been indifferent to God, or you would never have spent the night talking to him, honestly telling him what was in your heart and mind. Do you know the Christian word that describes what you have been doing? The word is 'prayer'. You have spent the night praying.

This insight completely changed the attitude of the hospice patient. Not long after his conversation with the chaplain, he died in peace, trusting the God who remains on speaking terms with us even when our only words for him are words of abuse." Roy Lawrence[144]

God answers prayer because he hears the cry of our hearts; because we dare to ask. James, in his apostolic letter, chides the early Christians bluntly: "You do not have, because you do not

Day 4

ask God" (James 4:2). The only prayer God cannot answer is the prayer we do not pray.

There is an interesting question raised by God's dramatic rescue of Daniel from the lions' den: *to whose prayer was God responding?* We are told that Daniel had a habit of daily prayer, but not that he prayed specifically for rescue. We are told, though, that *someone* did. King Darius, even as he is having Daniel thrown to the lions, says, "May your God, whom you serve continually, rescue you!" (Dan 6:16)

It is Darius who lies awake all night, anxious to know of Daniel's fate – and it is Darius himself who rushes to the pit at dawn to *ask his victim* if his God has rescued him. In Daniel 3:28 Nebuchadnezzar congratulates the three Hebrew rebels for defying a law he himself passed, but in Daniel 6:16 King Darius goes even further: *he defies his own decree to call on Yahweh.* Could it be that Daniel's dramatic escape from certain death was God's answer to the stumbling, desperate prayer of a pagan king? Strange things happen when ordinary people pray, and the potent cocktail of faith, desperation and a willingness to ask can bring change in the most unlikely of lives.

We will know that God is there for us in times of pressure when we have learned, in simple trust, to call on him. In coming to understand the workings of prayer, there is no substitute for the lessons learned in the apparent dead ends of desperation and radical dependence.

The spirituality of Daniel, through a consistent and continued commitment to prayer, places the presence and reality of God at the very heart of his life. Prayer is not an emergency procedure to be adopted when the going gets tough; it is effective precisely because it has been adopted and sustained whether the going is tough or not. Whatever else we might learn from the adventures of this 'holy hooligan' disrupting the smooth running of an empire, we should at the very least learn this: The pressures of life will not harm us if we are able, and willing, to know God's presence at the very centre of our lives.

"About twelve years ago, I was visiting an Orthodox monastery, and was taken to see one of the smaller and older chapels. It was a place intensely full of the memory and reality of prayer. The monk showing me around pulled the curtain from in front of the sanctuary, and inside was a plain altar and one simple picture of Jesus, darkened and rather undistinguished. But for some reason at that moment it was as if the veil of the temple was torn in two: I saw as I had never seen the simple fact of Jesus at the heart of all our words and worship, behind the curtain of our anxieties and our theories, our struggles and our suspicion. Simply there; nothing anyone can do about it, there he is as he has promised to be till the world's end. Nothing of value happens in the church that does not start from seeing him simply there in our midst, suffering and transforming our human disaster." Rowan Williams[145]

Question Time

This teaching block has suggested that it is by developing a habit of prayer in the ordinary run of life that we will have the right understanding of prayer in the extraordinary moments, when the pressure is on and we need God's rescue. Reflect on your own spiritual journey.

- Have there been times for you when the benefits of praying in the ordinary have been seen as you have faced the extraordinary?

- What styles and systems of prayer have you found most helpful; both in the everyday and in times of particular pressure and need?

- If you had the opportunity, tomorrow, to carve out a new routine of daily prayer and your home and work circumstances allowed you free reign, what would you opt to do to find God's daily presence?

Voices in Exile:
You catch my eye

You catch my eye
In the eye of the storm;
You hold ointment appointments
When hell's hornets swarm.
When I find no time for stillness
You tell me there's still time;
When my words are clashing symbols,
You are Reason,
Rhythm,
Rhyme.

You are the unexpected cheer that lifts my game;
In the vinegar and lemon juice of life,
You are champagne.

You are a bed of roses
On a crowded street;
A peppermint balm
To my blistered feet;
You are rich in rest,
When rest is radium-rare.
By cool pools you position me
With passion you petition me;
In fog and smog,
You re-condition my air.

You are the song that rises in my soul;
The coin that clatters in my begging bowl.

Like a goat's milk bath
To Cleopatra;
Like honey on the throat
To Frank Sinatra;
You surround me to astound me,
You soothe and smooth.

You are the stalker who is good for me;
The jailer who can set me free;
The trap and snare to bind me
Into love.

You who have refined me,
Come find me;
Mind me;
By grace grind me;
Bind me, gentle jailer,
Into love.[146]

In The Zone
Consider the place that prayer plays in the context of the Zone you are exploring.

- *Faith and a Changing World*
  Do the changing currents and contours of our culture call for new ways of exploring spirituality? What resources are there in the prayers of the past – throughout the church's history – to help us as we face a changing future?

- *Faith and the Developing World*
  How does the diversity of God's multi-coloured, multi-cultured, multi-national family help us as we build authentic spirituality for our Western exile? Are there lessons to be learned from the prayer lives of believers in cultures other than our own?

- *Faith and Devotional Life*
  What might the call for a *deeper* life of prayer and a *daily* life of prayer mean in your own devotional life? In praying for others, and for local, national and international needs, what resources do the patterns and passions of Daniel 9 have to offer?

- *Faith and Everyday Life*
  What are the ways in which you might develop a more effective daily routine of prayer? Is it realistic to aspire to a deeper life of prayer in the midst of a busy life in a hectic world? If it is, what decisions and determinations might this involve?

- *Faith and Family Life*
  What place should prayer have in the life of the family? Should individual prayer or household prayer be the priority? For those responsible for children, can we aspire to a deeper life of prayer for them or are they restricted to simple prayers until they're older?

- *Faith and Involvement*
  Is it possible to combine a busy life of public service with a dynamic life of private prayer, as Daniel seems to do? If it is, what kinds of tips, techniques and tools will help those trying to keep this balance?

- *Faith and Working Life*
  Is there a realistic role for prayer in the workplace? Should believers pray, as Daniel did, with their windows open (i.e. in full view of their colleagues) or are there times and places in which prayer is better kept a private practice?

Day 4

Voices in Exile:
Sokreaksa Himm – Praying the Psalms

(Sokreaksa S. Himm survived the killing fields of Cambodia. As a child, he saw his entire family – his 13 closest relations – killed by the Khmer Rouge. He eventually made his way to Canada, where he became a Christian and attended Bible college. But even in adult life, he was plagued by memories of the trauma he had lived through. By day he would be struck by sudden flashbacks, and by night graphic dreams would wake him, sweating and shaking all over. He describes how the Psalms, and especially Psalm 23, became a source of comfort and healing.)

I might never lose the sense of the presence of my enemies, but this affirmation of God's goodness reassures me. In this context I can pray about my fear, trusting in God's love and protection.

This psalm was also special to me in another way. One night when I was meditating on it, I seemed to see a picture of the cross with a ray of light on it. I didn't know how I saw the picture, but it was very real to me. I told some friends about this vision, and they said it was some kind of illusion, but I knew it was real. It was another source of comfort and reassurance.

Since I've been using this psalm for my evening meditation, my nightmares have left me: I haven't once dreamed of being hunted by the Khmer Rouge or the Thai soldiers. It seems as though my need for security and comfort while I sleep is met by this psalm, because I know I can trust God. I told some psychologists how I'd learned to deal with my nightmares by this method, and they didn't believe me. I admit that it doesn't sound very scientific, but I don't care. I tried the scientific advice, and it didn't work. The book of Psalms does work, and that's good enough for me.

It has worked for others, too. I have worked with many Cambodians who display all the symptoms of Post Traumatic Stress Disorder that I once had, and I have taught them the use of Psalm 23. Many of them have told me that it deals with their nightmares, and helps them to feel secure in the presence of the Lord.

… Since I have forgiven those who killed my family, my life has changed. The fire of hatred has gone from my heart and soul, though the bitterness has not been forgotten. By forgiving completely, I can move ahead, relying on God's healing power. Forgiveness has released me from the emotional torment that burned within me for years, and now my heart is lighter and my spirit has peace.[147]

Voices in Exile:
Bill Hybels – With dad in the boat…

When I was a young teenager learning to sail my dad's yacht, I'd often take a friend of my own age out on Lake Michigan. If I saw a threatening cloud formation coming our way, however, or if the winds began feeling a bit strong, I'd quickly take the sails down and head for shore. It was nice having a pal with me. The companionship was pleasant. But in a storm, my inexperienced crew would be no good to me at all.

Other times my dad and I would sail together. Again I'd take the helm, but with dad in the boat I eagerly looked for cloud formations and heavy winds. My dad had sailed across the Atlantic Ocean, had survived five days of hurricane and was able to handle anything Lake Michigan could throw at us. With him on board, I had both companionship and confidence.

… Companionship is wonderful. Even more wonderful is realising who your closest companion is: God almighty, the creator and sustainer of the universe, able to empower you to face anything that comes your way.[148]

Conclusion:
God meant it for good

Scholars have noted the many parallels between the life of Daniel and that of an earlier biblical hero, Joseph, whose story dominates twenty chapters of the book of Genesis and is foundational to Hebrew identity and culture. Just as Joseph was used by God as a foreigner in the courts of Egypt, so Daniel is used in Babylon. And just as Joseph was able to say to his brothers, who had cruelly abused him, that "God intended it for good" (Gen 50:20), so Daniel proves, at the end of his life, that the trauma of the exile has been made good in the purposes of God.

"In previous chapters, we had reason to note similarities between Daniel and Joseph. As we read the Joseph story with this principle in mind, we see again and again how God delivered him from the evil intentions of human beings. ... Joseph himself articulated the principle we are applying to the story in Daniel 6. After the death of Jacob, Joseph's brothers thought the time of their punishment for mistreating their brother had come. In response to their pleas for mercy, however, Joseph expressed his certainty concerning God's purposes in his suffering over the years: 'You intended to harm me, but God intended it for good to accomplish what is now being done, the saving of many lives.'" Tremper Longman[149]

The faith by which we are able to overcome the pressures heaped upon us – whatever their source – is the faith that tells us that God will bring to good every trial we endure. There is grief, but beyond it there is joy. The miracle of the God of Joseph and of Daniel is that in the face of the worst the world can throw at us, we will still be able to say God meant it for good. We can face our own pressures, and grieve for the pressures others face, because we know that the promise of God is all joy.

"There is work to be done in the present. There is grief work to be done in the present that the future may come. There is mourning to be done for those who do not know of the deathliness of their situation. There is mourning to be done with those who know pain and suffering and lack the power or freedom to bring it to speech. The saying is a harsh one, for it sets grief as the precondition of joy. It announces that those who have not cared enough to grieve will not know joy." Walter Brueggemann[150]

Day 4

Voices in Exile:
Books to read in Babylon

Imprisoned in Iran (YWAM Publishing, 2000) is Dan Bauman's own account of his arrest and imprisonment in Tehran. An 'ordinary American' travelling with YWAM, Bauman was plunged into the horror of a high-security Iranian jail when he was falsely accused of espionage. A gripping story in itself, this book is also an insightful journal of faith: honest about the despair and fear that can grip us, but passionate about the hope that God brings. A powerful testimony from a Daniel of today.

Bill Hybel's ***Too Busy Not to Pray: Slowing Down to be With God*** (Inter-Varsity Press, 1988) has been in print for several years, but has the staying power to stand as something of a contemporary classic. Honest, perceptive and pastorally-driven, this book will leave you in no doubt as to the central place of prayer in Christian discipleship and growth. It will give you plenty of inspiration and ideas to kick start or renew a commitment to prayer at the heart of your daily experience.

David Adam, vicar of Holy Island, is well known as a passionate advocate of Celtic spirituality. ***The Cry of the Deer*** (SPCK, 1987) is one of his best explorations of the prayers of this ancient tradition. Based on the hymn attributed to St Patrick – known both as 'The Deer's Cry' and as 'St Patrick's Breastplate' – this is an illustrated journey through an understanding of prayer that holds confidently to the presence of God in the real world of everyday experience.

Rhythms of Grace: Finding Intimacy with God in a Busy Life (Kingsway, 2004) by Tony Horsfall is a new exploration of the contemplative approach to prayer. The author speaks very honestly about his own need, after many years of evangelical and charismatic spirituality, to find a way of prayer that would take him 'deeper into God'. He challenges his reader to break out of busyness and burn-out and to find strength in God's rhythms for life, exploring long-established traditions of prayer and personal devotion.

The Tears of My Soul (Monarch, 2003) by Sokreaksa S. Himm is a powerful story of the triumph of forgiveness over hatred. Sokreaksa was the only member of his family to escape from Cambodia's killing fields, where he witnessed the murder of his 13 closest relations. Alone, afraid and deeply traumatised, he grew up in the shadow of this horrific atrocity: but he learned to forgive, and to find the peace of God for his life. A fast-moving story told with honesty and integrity, Sokreaksa's own account of his life is a resounding assertion that the presence of God can be found even in the most desperate circumstances of life.

Tortured for Christ (Living Sacrifice Book Company, 1967, 1998) by Richard Wurmbrand was first published in 1967 and recently re-issued in an updated edition. A personal account of imprisonment and torture in Romania in the very worst of the Communist era, *Tortured for Christ* is a moving spiritual journal by a pastor of deep wisdom and faith. One of history's most moving accounts of a faith that can withstand the worst of circumstances – and of a love that overcomes the greatest of fears.

Tried by Fire (Monarch, 2003)*,* edited and translated by Anna Lee Stangl of Christian Solidarity Worldwide, is predominantly the verbatim testimonies of seven Peruvian Christians, all of whom have been unjustly imprisoned in recent years: caught up in their government's bloody war against the Shining Path guerrillas. The testimonies are a moving account of God's power and courage amongst the poorest of the poor, and of love's capacity to make of the worst of situations an opportunity for grace and kindness to be shown.

Matt Roper's ***Street Girls: Hope on the Streets of Brazil*** (Authentic, 2001) tells the astounding and at times overwhelming story of one young man's commitment to some of the world's most abused young people. A stirring testimony to the power of prayer in hopeless situations, and to the possibility of change in the darkest of lives, this moving book is probably one of the best portraits available of what it might truly mean to 'dare to be a Daniel' in today's world.

Light Force – The Only Hope for the Middle East (Hodder & Stoughton, 2004), written by Brother Andrew and Al Janssen, brings the story of 'God's Smuggler' right up to date. Brother Andrew chronicles his travels through the Middle East over many years, meeting men both of peace and of violence on all sides of the conflict. This is a challenging and provocative journal from the man who has done more than any other in recent years to put the needs of the persecuted church on to the agenda of the evangelical community.

Day 5

Power:
Faith in a faithful God

Outline of the Day:

Introduction: Power

Overview: Daniel 4 and 5

Teaching Block 1:   page 89

Sovereign power: a faithful God at work in the unfolding of history

Question Time

In The Zone

Teaching Block 2:   page 94

Power to serve: a faithful God seen in the selflessness of faithful service

Question Time

In The Zone

Teaching Block 3:   page 101

Power to thrive: a faithful God for the long haul of a faithful life

Question Time

In The Zone

Conclusion: Faith transforms the experience of exile

Books

Introduction: Power

"In the white blaze of this kingdom of his there was to be no property, no privilege, no pride and no precedence; no motive indeed and no reward but love. Is it any wonder that men were dazzled and blinded and cried out against him?" H.G. Wells[151]

A question hovers beneath the surface of the book of Daniel in both its story-based and vision-based chapters: *What is the source of true power?* This question comes sharply into focus in chapters 4 and 5 as Daniel personally confronts two kings – in the eyes of the world the most powerful men on the planet. The source,

operation, character and tone of *true power* is one of the deep themes of Daniel's story.

But the answer to the question, *What is the source of true power?*, is not given as a *what* but as a *who*. Power for life and witness is rooted, for Daniel, in the character of God himself. It is because he is sovereign that he has all power, and because he is faithful that his power is made available. Daniel experiences the power of God in Babylon, because he has faith in a faithful God.

Key verse:
How great are his signs, how mighty his wonders! His kingdom is an eternal kingdom; his dominion endures from generation to generation.
Daniel 4:3

Overview: Daniel 4 and Daniel 5

In the two 'power encounters' of chapters 4 and 5, we see Daniel confronting two different rulers, separated by some 60 years. There are subtle but significant differences in the ways in which the two rulers are portrayed. Nebuchadnezzar's treatment in the text is not without sympathy. He is an all-powerful dictator, and has crushed the nation of Israel, but his character is not beyond redemption. In his later years, when God confronts his pride and he responds, he experiences a kind of conversion.

"His overweening pride was rightfully exposed, and he was shown to be a brute beast on his own power; even his sanity was a gift from God. His humiliating experience compelled him to look at God again, and he was restored to his former dignity." Tremper Longman[152]

At the end of his story, Nebuchadnezzar is presented as the king *repentant and restored*. By the end of chapter 3 he has come to recognise the power of Daniel's God and to respect him; but he is still playing 'power games' in his own life. By the end of chapter 4 though, this is over; his recognition of Yahweh is complete and he is content simply to worship.

"This king now has a discernment and a vision of God's true governance of the world." Walter Brueggemann[153]

Belshazzar comes to the throne 23 years after the death of Nebuchadnezzar and is portrayed, in contrast, as a king *resistant and rejected*. A corrupt and immoral tyrant, he is presented in this narrative as beyond redemption.

"Belshazzar's first and final episode in the stories of Daniel is marked by his arrogance, blasphemy, idolatry." Tremper Longman[154]

The king's decision to use the goblets taken from the Jerusalem temple – and kept safe for over 60 years in the treasure house of Babylon – is symbolic of both his disdain for Yahweh and his own depravity.

"Belshazzar goes even further in his sacrilege. He is not only committing blasphemy, he combines it with idolatry. Here is where his profanation surpasses that of Nebuchadnezzar. He uses God's holy goblets to toast the lifeless idols of his own religion. He spits in God's eye, as it were, and then he goes over to a statue that he himself has created (v.4) and expects that lifeless hunk to protect him from what is to come." Tremper Longman[155]

Day 5

God's judgement on Belshazzar is swift and severe, and the text wastes little time in sympathy for him: his defeat and death are recorded in less than half a sentence. Daniel has no need of his proffered riches and reward, because he knows how fragile, in the context of God's sovereign power, the emperor's destiny is.

"... perhaps having read the inscription already, Daniel knows that the reward means nothing. The king has nothing really to give." Tremper Longman[156]

For all the differences between these two accounts, and the characters of the kings central to them, the essential meaning of the stories is the same. Even though these men are amongst the most powerful figures on earth; even though in the world in which Daniel lives they have absolute power – yet still the sovereign God is more powerful.

"There can be little doubt that the author of Daniel 5 wrote it, and intended it to be read, with chapter 4 in mind. The reference to Nebuchadnezzar in v.2, and then in v.11, prepares the way for an extended comparison between Belshazzar and his 'father'... ." Ernest Lucas[157]

These stories present alternative views of the nature of true power.

- On the one hand, the power of the king(s). This is a political power, imposed by military might, administered with unquestioned authority and maintained through fear. This is power as history tends to perceive it and as the majority of people accept it: the kind of power by which our lives are shaped and dominated.

- On the other hand, though, there is another power – the power that comes from knowing God. This is a more personal power, accessed through prayer, administered in weakness and maintained through trust in a sovereign God. This is a power rarely noticed by historians and unseen by many people: but it is the kind of power by which history is truly made.

Through the confident faith by which he clings to the sovereignty of his God, and the rich wisdom expressed in his life, Daniel is able to show that the power that comes from knowing God is ultimately stronger and more lasting than even the greatest political power.

The experience of exile that begins with the loss of power, ends in the discovery of a greater power still.

What can we learn from these encounters?

When we were introduced to Daniel in chapter 1, it was in the context of a loss of power. On their journey from Jerusalem to Babylon, Daniel and his friends said goodbye to the freedoms and privileges by which they had tended to measure the power of their God. They were powerless before a world-crushing empire. Daniel in particular is subsequently called to stand before a succession of Babylonian rulers: he is the pawn facing the king; the stateless exile before the focus of all authority. The very definition of powerlessness stands before the personification of power. Like Joseph and Moses before him, Daniel has no currency to rely on but faith. But it is in just this context that he discovers the greater power of his God. In the uneven contest of the emperor and the exile, it is the exile – odds-on favourite to lose – who carries the day.

Through over seventy years in Babylon, Daniel discovers that God's power is:

- *rooted in God's faithfulness*. He is the source of all power because he is the king of the whole earth – as powerful in Babylon as he ever was in Jerusalem.

- *characterised by faithful service,* not by pomp and prestige. To the humble exile, captive in a foreign court and stripped of the visible signs of wordly power, God's greater power is revealed.

- *seen in the long haul of a faithful life.* God's power makes it possible to thrive in an alien land. Even without the exile being brought to an end, the superior power of Yahweh is displayed.

Teaching Block 1:
Sovereign power: a faithful God at work in the unfolding of history

1.1 God's power is made available to God's saints
1.2 God's power is released through the workings of faith
1.3 God's power is essential to God's mission
1.4 God's power is at work throughout the world

"The content of Nebuchadnezzar's testimony is the nature of the sovereignty of the Most High God. The one who claims to rule 'people of every race, nation and language' acknowledges that there is a higher rule, which is mighty and everlasting. The story, which begins with the words of a mighty human ruler, will explore the relationship between human and divine sovereignty." Ernest Lucas[158]

The first and loudest message of Daniel's 'power encounters' is that God, not the king, is in charge. Whatever power the kings of Babylon might display, God's power is greater. However big their empire might be, God's kingdom is bigger. However unshakeable their dominion might appear, it is nothing compared to the dominion of God. Jesus places himself explicitly in this same tradition. He adopts the title 'Son of Man', derived from Daniel, and when he stands before Pilate, just as Daniel stood before the kings of Babylon, he makes the same proclamation – "You would have no power over me if it were not given to you from above" (John 19:11). All earthly power – whether that of the pagan kings of the sixth century exile or the Roman generals of the first century occupation of Palestine – is subject to the sovereignty of God.

The ground and anchor of our faith is not the strength of our feelings: it is the faithfulness of God himself.

It is relatively easy for us to appreciate this truth in the lives of Daniel and Jesus, whom we view and admire from a distance. When power encounters come closer to home, it is perhaps harder to proclaim God's sovereign power. Can the generation that lived through World War 2 say Hitler would have had no power had it not been given him 'from above'? Could we use those words of Stalin, of Saddam Hussein, of Pinochet?

The Bible would insist that we can, and must: not to sanction oppression or to justify unjustifiable regimes; but to assert beyond all other claims that no dictator, no atrocity, no evil, no holocaust can eclipse the central truth that God is in control. God's power may be hidden from our sight: but no cloud can change the fact that God's power shines. This is crucial to the biblical understanding of power, because it is only by faith in a sovereign God that:

- the exiles of the sixth century BC could press on through their ordeal;

- the Jews of the second century BC could hold on to hope against the efforts of Antiochus Epiphanes to wipe out their faith;

- the Christian churches of the first and second centuries could push on for growth against the opposition both of the Jewish leaders and, in time, the Roman Empire;

- prophets, preachers and people of prayer in every time and culture, no matter how clouded their skies, can engage in God's purposes, confident in the certainties of his sovereign power.

Daniel's portrait of a power rooted in the sovereignty of God resonates with the wider witness of Scripture, and establishes the key parameters of the workings of God's power in our lives.

Day 5

1.1 God's power is made available to God's saints

- The sovereign God, who is so big that the movements of nations and empires are as nothing to him, is prepared to manifest his power *in, for and on behalf of* his willing servants.

The audacity of Daniel's witness in Babylon is not only that he asserts God's power over history – and over his imperial captors – but that he also claims to *have access* to that power. The book of Daniel makes no sense whatsoever if the supernatural intervention of God in the exiles' lives is taken out of it.

Jim Cymbala, pastor of the dynamic Brooklyn Tabernacle in New York, insists that this same power remains available to God's saints today.

"That power may come in the form of wisdom, an idea you desperately need and can't come up with yourself. It may come in the form of courage greater than you could ever muster. It may come in the form of confidence or perseverance, uncommon staying power, a changed attitude towards a spouse or child or parent, changed circumstances, maybe even outright miracles. However it comes, God's prevailing power is released in the lives of people who pray." Bill Hybels[159]

Centuries after Daniel, the Apostle John would sum up this same dynamic of power in words of encouragement to a persecuted church: "The one who is in you is greater than the one who is in the world." (1 John 4:4)

In his faithfulness to us, God is able and willing to fulfil his promise that "you will receive power when the Holy Spirit comes on you; and you will be my witnesses." (Acts 1:8)

1.2 God's power is released through the workings of faith

- It is through the exercise of *faith* that the power of the sovereign God is brought into our everyday lives.

Through the humiliation of Nebuchadnezzar and the judgement of Belshazzar, and through Daniel's central role in both, we learn that it is in issues of power that *faith comes into focus*. Faith cannot be held captive to a fantasy world that denies the evident realities of life: it must be tested in the real world, where lives are made or marred by the uses and abuses of power. Biblical faith is never portrayed in isolation from the world, but always in contact with it and often in confrontation; whether with the personal power of sin, disease and adversity, with the political power of a king or leader, or with the principalities and powers behind the facts of history. It is by the 'shield of faith' that we are able to 'extinguish all the flaming arrows of the evil one' (Eph 6:16). Particularly in the gospels, *faith* is represented as the corollary of God's *power*. Even the tiniest shred of true faith has the power to impact the world.

"I tell you the truth, if you have faith as small as a mustard seed, you can say to this mountain, 'Move from here to there' and it will move. Nothing will be impossible for you." (Matt 17:20)

Throughout Scripture, godly power – the power that is accessed by faith and impacts the world against the odds – is contrasted to the worldly power of human strength and achievement.

"When I came to you, brothers, I did not come with eloquence or superior wisdom as I proclaimed to you the testimony about God. For I resolved to know nothing while I was with you except Jesus Christ and him crucified. I came to you in weakness and fear, and with much trembling. My message and my preaching were not with wise and persuasive words, but with a demonstration of the Spirit's power, <u>so that your faith might not rest on men's wisdom, but on God's power</u>." (1 Cor 2:1, emphasis added)

A youth group in the West Midlands recently put together an audio-visual presentation on this power that is 'made perfect in weakness'. One of the images they used came from the film *The Perfect Storm*. It showed a single fishing boat, alone, climbing the slope of a wave so huge that the boat seemed the size of a flea. All around were the signs of a colossal storm. The boat was surely lost. It was an image that was instantly recognisable to anyone who has ever been dwarfed by the scale of the problems they face. But beside it, these young people had written:

"Tired of telling God how big your storm is? Try telling the storm how big your God is."

It is by *our* faith in *God's* faithfulness that the storms we face in life are calmed and conquered. Faith is not a commodity that we spend to buy God's favour – it is not a skill we can 'turn on'. Faith grows in us as our character grows: it is an aspect of becoming Christlike. As we respond to God's faithfulness to us, and seek to become more like him, we find faith more and more at work in us. It was because Daniel was godly in character that God so resoundingly vindicated his faith.

1.3 God's power is essential to God's mission

- It is only by the power of God that the purposes of God can be fulfilled.

It is the unified message of Scripture that God's *mission* is dependent on God's *power*. We are called to be *importers* of God's power before we even dare to be *imparters* of God's message. The words, works and wonders of God's life in the world are to be enjoined wholly and solely by means of his power. In a previous generation, the great evangelist DL Moody wrote:

"Unless He attend the word in power, vain will be the attempt in preaching it. Human eloquence or persuasiveness of speech are the mere trappings of the dead. If the living Spirit be absent, the prophet may preach to the bones in the valley, but it must be the breath from heaven that will cause the slain to live."[160]

Jim Cymbala takes up the same call for the contemporary church – not just in its preaching, but in every aspect of its life and mission.

"God says that when we call, he will answer. ... We have too many mere technicians who are only stressing methodology, and they are increasingly invading the church. The answer is not in any human methodology. The answer is in the power of the Holy Spirit."[161]

The outpouring of God's Spirit at Pentecost, promised through the prophets and longed for by God's people through all time, is a resounding assertion that it is only in God's power that the church can live and grow.

"Then he spells it out, 'Mortal boy, these bones are the Jews. They admit, "We're dried up. Hope's long gone. We're like scattered skeletons." So tell them, "This is Awesome God's message: my people, I'm going to exhume you from your graves, bring your rotting bones back to Israel. If I've opened your graves and brought your bones back, you'll know I'm in charge. My Spirit in you will pump breath into your lungs. You'll come to life and live in your own homeland. Then you'll be sure that I'm running things round here, and what I say goes,"' says God." (Ezek 37:11–14, The Street Bible)

The driving force of God's mission in the world, the power by which it is sustained and carried, is not found in our determination nor our effort. It is rooted in the faithfulness of God, who has promised, and will deliver.

Day 5

1.4 God's power is at work throughout the world

- The power of God which is at work in our lives is also at work throughout his world.

It is in this larger perspective of God's sovereignty in history that the mission of God in the world must be grasped. God is at work in the church; he is at work in your life, but he is also at work in history, bringing the world to its appointed destiny. There is a scope to the mission of God that we often fail to grasp. But *Daniel didn't fail to grasp it,* he is lifted beyond the narrow view of exile to the broad and limitless horizons of a God who is sovereign over history.

"It is necessary to correct the tendency to base mission on a few selected texts from the New Testament. What has to be grasped is God's purpose for humankind as revealed in Scripture, and the missionary thrust of the whole history of salvation. This will throw new light on the nature of mission." Samuel Escobar[162]

Whatever our own present experience – prosperity or persecution, expansion or exile – the truth is that God's church is growing across the world. The appointed time, when every tribe and tongue and nation and power will celebrate the victory of Christ, is drawing closer.

"The fact is that the gospel is making headway among the many tribes, nations and languages – that it is indeed making more headway among them than among the dominant cultures of the North Atlantic. The question is not whether there will be a multicultural church. Rather, the question is whether those who have become so accustomed to seeing the gospel expressed only or primarily in terms of those dominant cultures will be able to participate in the life of the multicultural church that is already a reality." Justo Gonzales[163]

The faithfulness of God is not seen in our lives alone, but in all the colourful diversity of his work in the world.

Question Time

The power of God is rooted in his sovereignty over all the earth, and is made available to his saints by the presence of his Holy Spirit.

- Have there been times in your life when you have assumed that the 'enemy' you face – whether oppression, sickness, debt or other difficulties – is more powerful than the God you serve?

- What does it mean to expect the power of God to be at work in your situation?

- How do life and mission carried out *with* the power of God differ from life and mission carried out *without* his power?

In The Zone

What is the place for the empowering of the Holy Spirit in the Zone you are exploring?

- *Faith and a Changing World*
  How are the changing demands and expectations of our culture likely to impact our understanding of the workings of God's power? What are the new ways the Spirit-empowered life might be expressed in the new, emerging contexts of our culture?

- *Faith and the Developing World*
  How does belief in the sovereignty of God help those whose Christian life is lived out on the losing side of social development? What is the place of the Spirit's empowerment amongst the poor and needy?

- *Faith and Devotional Life*
  How does trust in God's sovereignty impact the devotional life? Is there a particular place for the empowerment of the Spirit in the growth and practice of prayer in our lives?

- *Faith and Everyday Life*
  What are the circumstances in which we need to know that the God we worship is in ultimate control of our lives? How does the empowerment of the Spirit change the lives we lead day by day?

- *Faith and Family Life*
  Does the belief that God is in control change the way we view the pressure faced in the family? What role does the power of the Holy Spirit have in our families, households and homes?

- *Faith and Involvement*
  How does the sovereignty of God over all history – the assertion that all power is exercised by his permission – change the way we view public and political opponents? What difference might the empowering of the Spirit make to a life of public service?

- *Faith and Working Life*
  What kinds of problems arising in the workplace can seem more powerful than God? How does faith in the God who is in control, and who makes his power available to us, change the way we view tough times at work?

Day 5

Teaching Block 2:
Power to serve: a faithful God seen in the selflessness of faithful service

2.1 The way we read Christian history
2.2 The way we carry out God's mission in the world
2.3 The way we understand and practise leadership
2.4 The way we embrace and express the message of the cross

When the pope visited Peru in the early 1990s, groups representing the indigenous peoples of the Andes worked together to write to him. Reflecting on the long and complex history of Christian mission in their region, in which the power of the cross had so often been allied to the power of the gun, they presented him with the gift of a Bible. In the letter that accompanied the gift, they said:

"We peoples of the Andean countries of America decided to avail of your visit in order to give you back your Bible, because in five centuries it has brought neither love, nor peace, nor justice. Please take your Bible and give it back to our oppressors because they clearly need its moral precepts more than we do."[164]

It is perhaps the most painful legacy of the Christendom era that the name of Christ has so often been allied to the power of force and coercion. Christendom has not been kind to those who do not readily accept its views, and the power by which the gospel has been preached has not always been the power of a self-emptying carpenter. In Daniel's context, the confrontations with the kings of Babylon not only contrast their 'dominion' with the sovereign dominion of God, they also offer a second contrast: between the power of these kings, with all their pomp, wealth and military strength, and the power of Daniel – the dispossessed exile dependent solely on the presence of his God. The contrast is graphic and dramatic, and God's sympathies are unambiguous: he is not impressed by the evident power of empires and armies – he is present with the powerless exile.

Because Daniel's faith is invested in the faithfulness of God, because the source of his

personal power is a *who* and not a *what,* his expectation is that God's character will be reflected in the workings of his power. God's loving faithfulness in our lives is not only the *source* of the power that we need: it is also our *model* for the exercise of power.

"Daniel urges Nebuchadnezzar to accept a radically different characterization of power and of reality (Dan 4:27). Domination is translated into righteousness and the practice of caring fidelity (cf. Mark 10:42–44). Control is transformed into mercy for the oppressed, all those on whose backs the empire was built." Walter Brueggemann[165]

Captain America or Hosea: what kind of power for today's world?
In the central museum of Lahore, Pakistan, there is a fine bronze statue of Queen Victoria that once stood at the very heart of the city's biggest crossroads. The statue has been well preserved in all but one detail. The orb that her majesty holds in her hand was originally topped by a cross, but this has been broken off. Commentators suggest this act of vandalism almost certainly reflects the well-documented Muslim hatred of the cross: but does it also serve as a reminder that the cross cannot be used as a symbol of military conquest, political authority and imperial domination? If the chequered history of Christendom, and of the British Empire, teaches us nothing else, it should warn us of the dangers of confusing these two ideas of power.

Robert Jewett and John Shelton Lawrence, in *Captain America and the Crusade Against Evil,* explore these same important questions in a North American context. They trace this long-standing tradition of 'redemptive violence' and analyse its particular impact on US foreign policy.

"Two paths thus lie open to those who would reform American society today, or take up her calling to serve the world. There is the way of redemptive violence, which may take the form of the great revolution or the great crusade: this path promises to shatter injustice with a righteous fury punishing the evildoers, emancipating those who have been exploited, and making the world safe for virtue. But there is also the way of redemptive love: its promise is less clear-cut, and it leads to much less predictable results. For when love is enacted, people become free. New impulses awaken that no one can master ahead of time. So this is the way for the audacious and the large in spirit, those who can live without idols and face an uncertain future unafraid."[166]

The point here is not to single out American military action as history's only example of the marriage of spiritual and temporal power, or even as its worst. All the great empires of Christendom have faced the temptation to add God's name and authority to their military, commercial and political power. Very often, it is images drawn from the Bible itself that are cited to justify this marriage. The military victories of Israel over her pagan neighbours, much aided by Yahweh's presence and power, are re-read in the context of whatever battle the nation or empire is fighting. In a similar way the apocalyptic language of Daniel and Revelation, with its open confrontation of good against evil, may be cited in support of a particular campaign.

"The confusion in the United States and probably other Western democracies arises because some Christians insist that their country is the modern equivalent to Israel. However it cannot be argued too strongly that there are and can be no modern equivalents of Israel. There is no such thing as a 'Christian nation', except in the sense of a nation where most of the inhabitants happen to be Christian at that particular historical moment. ... Christians do not fight for their beliefs by assaulting or killing but by dying." Tremper Longman[167]

Where Scripture is used to 'baptise' the use of violence in God's name, the more subtle message of Daniel and of exile is missed: God's power is demonstrated as a *different kind of power* to the imperial power of crusade and conquest. One of the key theological functions of the exile in Israel's history was precisely this – to demonstrate that the power and presence of God were not inseparably tied to the military and political victory of Israel. This 'growth-point' in the theological maturity of Israel is then taken further by the New Testament, when the Messiah turns out to be as far from a conquering military hero as it is possible to get. Jesus is the king who conquers not by violence but by love. He does the very thing *'that kings cannot do and yet remain kings'*[168] – he willingly surrenders his power.

Alan Storkey, who has dedicated three decades to understanding and practising a Christian approach to politics, suggests that this embracing of another kind of power is the central reality of the politics of Jesus.

"In the Gospels, we are presented with a perspective on power so radical and disturbing that few have understood or come to terms with it even today. For Jesus attacks the very notion of power as <u>control over</u>. Throughout human history, men have sought to control others, seeing that as the way to make their own lives more affluent, secure and free from work. Conquest, enslavement, control systems, state buttressing taxes, docile populations and manipulation have been normal parts of this cultural complex. Its costs are staggering. Human history is littered with castles, wars, slave trading, refugees, impoverishment, futile work, destruction, spy systems, bombing and other systems of effort which have resulted from the human need for <u>control over</u>. England loses its oaks to make battleships. Chechnya is flattened in a fight for control. Hitler devastates the lives of hundreds of millions in a need to dominate. Bombs are the most efficient way of wasting power ever invented. Although we may focus on the worst examples, the acceptance of <u>control over</u> is ordinary in the lives of many people and states. But what if this idiom is a great human mistake? This unthinkable truth Jesus has presented to us." Alan Storkey[169]

Day 5

For Jewett and Lawrence, the great orator of redemptive love in the Old Testament is the prophet Hosea, who denounced the violent behaviour of the house of Israel and promised a redemption that would come not through violence but through love. It is this promise that is fulfilled in Jesus.

"The passionate love of God came to earth, full of sensual, yearning, creative power. Jesus expressed love to people obsessed by the mystique of violence, as well as to those suffering under its brutal impact. It proved as redemptive as Hosea had promised. Small groups of restored persons began to emerge, and they reached out to others in their violence-prone society, with a vigour and joy which only love can produce."[170]

The implications of this other kind of power are not only that we worship a crucified God, but that we are called to be like him: to serve, not dominate. The whole profile of the Christian gospel in the world should be marked by this DNA of self-giving love.

This will have an impact on the way we read Christian history.

2.1 The way we read Christian history

- Issues of power and powerlessness, and of the kind of power we associate with the name of Christ, are central to our understanding of the history of Christianity in the world.

Historians have noted that in the heroic early years of the spread of Christianity its members were predominantly the poor and the powerless. The humble background of Jesus himself was matched by that of his first followers.

"[Jesus'] background was that of hard-working country people. Members of his own family are mentioned in Christian documents up to the third century. They seem to have remained fairly humble peasant farmers. And it was among such people that he found his disciples." Bamber Gascoigne[171]

This remained the dominant pattern for many years, as the Christian faith was transmitted hand-to-hand across the empire.

"... the majority of Christians were simple folk with little education. The church was not a bearer of culture. As a matter of fact, it was held in contempt by the vast majority of the cultured citizens of the Empire." David Bosch[172]

The implications of this are not that the powerful, the rich, the influential and the strong have no place in the church: but that it is not by earthly power, wealth, influence and strength that the gospel grows. The church was born amongst exiles, but has it too often taken on the trappings of empire? Raised up to be Daniel, have we chosen rather to be Nebuchadnezzar?

"... we must be honest and acknowledge that the truth has been used to manipulate, condemn, repress, restrict and oppress others in illegitimate ways. And we do not have to go back to theological arguments of the past that led to Jewish pogroms, to people who tried to resist civil rights, or to the support of apartheid in the name of the faith. Christianity is being used in the present to promote non-biblical models of the family, the relationships of the sexes, destructive attitudes towards people of 'alternative lifestyles', and so forth." Tremper Longman[173]

2.2 The way we carry out God's mission in the world

- Questions of power affect not only *what* we do for God in the world, but *how* we do it.

In his book on Christian leadership and ministry, Ian Cowley characterises the whole basis and ethos of servant-ministry in the following terms:

"Wait on God – Go in faith – Go empty-hand-ed." [174]

We are used to noting that this style of mission has not always been present in our history, but are we less adept at evaluating our own contemporary methods? Dan Drápal, a church leader in Prague, recently assessed the impact of Western missionaries coming into the Czech Republic. Both Czech and Slovakia saw a massive influx of Anglo-Saxon missionaries in the wake of the collapse of Communism; but 10 years on, an assessment of their efforts by local believers does not make comfortable reading.

"It was very common that some people coming from the West wanted to perform some drama, or hold a meeting. They turned to us to arrange it. We were supposed to organize all the permits, to rent a hall, to arrange and distribute the leaflets – they generously paid for it, performed their act – and went back home. Then we received their newsletter about how they 'did a mission campaign' in Eastern Europe. They did not bother to consider if their activity is really worthwhile, what its real impact was, if it was really the thing we need, and if we would not have been able to do the same thing better if we had the money." Dan Drápal[175]

The temptation to use superior wealth and power in the cause of mission is there for us whenever we engage in evangelism.

"Churches are free to choose the ways they consider best to announce the gospel to different people in different circumstances. But these options are never neutral. Every methodology illustrates or betrays the gospel we announce. In all communications of the gospel, power must be subordinate to love."[176]

The alternative is a form of mission and evangelism that is marked by servanthood, by listening and by love.

"The gentle rule of Jesus has overcome and judges the rule of kings, princes, generals, the rich and the mighty. Recognizing this in the middle of persecution and a dominant vicious Roman Empire was almost impossible, but slowly the good news that the Lamb is on the throne has filtered out. ... The old Messianic hope of a victory over the Romans is dismissed as irrelevant. The only power the disciples will receive is the power of the Holy Spirit, the Counsellor, God's Spirit of Truth, subduing the lying ego, and their task is to be witnesses to the gentle good news of Jesus." Alan Storkey[177]

2.3 The way we understand and practise leadership

- Leaders, more than anyone, need to decide what *kind of power* they will exercise in the fulfilment of their calling.

Not only in mission, but in the whole arena of leadership, the 'other kind of power' demonstrated in Daniel, Hosea and Jesus calls for deep reflection on our ways of operating.

"In a world where many leaders are focussed on their own self enhancement, projected image and drive to control, Jesus teaches us another way. It is a way of being powerful when you are weak, tough when you're soft and huge when you are small. It is absolutely subversive of the model given to us by a self-besotted world." Viv Thomas[178]

Nebuchadnezzar and Belshazzar represent an understanding of leadership that has shaped world history, and remains the dominant understanding: that leadership offers a place of privilege and power for the leader. Jesus models something very different, a servant leadership grounded in humility, exercising influence by love and nurture rather than coercion and control.

"I often hear Christian leaders tell what God has been saying to them in their times of meditation and study and prayer and I'm often amazed. He tells them the most profound, eloquent things. All I seem to ever hear is: Rob, get out of my way." Rob Bell[179]

Day 5

2.4 The way we embrace and express the message of the cross

- Issues of power and powerlessness are central to our grasp of the meaning of the cross.

"How are we to work out the lordship of Christ over all of life while maintaining the autonomy of the world, or at least without seeking a return to a situation in which the church rules the world? How can the church be involved in politics without recreating Christendom? The answer is to go back to the cross." Tim Chester[180]

Centrally, this understanding of 'a different kind of power' will shape our view of the cross: driving us to redeem this all-important symbol both from its trivialisation as a cultural artefact and from its appropriation as a symbol of earthly power.

"The cross loses its meaning if it is used like a charm to escape reality – or if it becomes so overlaid with gold and silver that it is only a thing of beauty. The cross is the promise that God cares and is involved with us in all of life, and there is nowhere where He has not been. The cross is the way to glory." David Adam[181]

David Smith writes movingly of this paradox of history, whereby those who claim the cross as system and symbol so often live as if it had no power.

"As an evangelical who wishes to confess the centrality of the cross in discipleship, theology and mission, I find myself asking whether, despite all our protestations that the death of Christ lies at the heart of our understanding of the Gospel, we have not treated it in ways that have eroded its power and glory. How has it happened that people who speak with such conviction and assurance about the atonement often show so little evidence in daily life, or in interpersonal relationships, of a 'crucified mind'? Why are orthodox Christian churches and organisations, with belief in the atonement of Christ enshrined in doctrinal statements that are binding on members, so often riven by ugly divisions resulting from

human pride, anger and intolerance? ... Doctrinal formulations concerning the atonement provide no guarantee in themselves that those affirming them will live their lives beneath the shadow of the cross." David Smith[182]

As a symbol alone, the cross will not change us. No matter how often we look at it, wear it, speak of it, sing of it or preach it, the way of the cross doesn't change us until we choose to live it. If we know that God is both the source of our power and the model by which we should exercise power, we will expect loving faithfulness to be the mark of all our dealings with the world.

How might the world be changed by a movement of contemporary Christians who grasp the truth that faith gives access to another kind of power – who redeem the cross from being a system and symbol and make of it, instead, a chosen path? What if instead of admiring, honouring and analysing the self-emptying of Jesus, we chose one day to follow his example?

"Think of yourselves the way Christ Jesus thought of himself. He had equal status with God but didn't think so much of himself that he had to cling to the advantages of that status no matter what. Not at all. When the time came, he set aside the privileges of deity and took on the status of a slave, became __human__! Having become human, he stayed human. It was an incredibly humbling process. He didn't claim special privileges. Instead, he lived a selfless, obedient life and then died a selfless, obedient death—and the worst kind of death at that: a crucifixion.

Because of that obedience, God lifted him high and honoured him far beyond anyone or anything, ever, so that all created beings in heaven and on earth—even those long ago dead and buried—will bow in worship before this Jesus Christ, and call out in praise that he is the Master of all, to the glorious honor of God the Father." (Phil 2:5–11, The Message)

Question Time

This teaching block has suggested that the contrast between Daniel and the Babylonian kings points to 'a different kind of power', and that this should shape and mark Christian conduct in the world. Reflecting on your own view of history, and of the world today, ask yourself:

- What examples can you think of where these two different ways of looking at power have been confused, and what has the result of this been?

- What are the areas in your own daily experience in which you are being called to conquer not by violence but by love?

- How might a commitment to operate by an understanding of power that seeks to serve rather than to dominate change the way we function as a church?

In The Zone

Consider the impact that a different understanding of power might bring in the Zone you are exploring.

- *Faith and a Changing World*
  How are the uses and abuses of power significant to the changing contours of our society and culture? What are the areas in which a power that serves might significantly impact our society?

- *Faith and the Developing World*
  What does the impact of Western missionary initiatives on the developing world have to say about the proper use of power? Are there lessons to be learned from those on the receiving end of mission?

- *Faith and Devotional Life*
  Where do the concepts of *relinquishing* power and *receiving* God's power fit in to the life of the praying disciple? How might the self-emptying (*kenosis*) of Jesus be a model for our devotional lives?

- *Faith and Everyday Life*
  What are the areas in which power is exercised in the everyday activities of our lives? How might the adoption of a power that serves impact our Christian behaviour, our evangelism and our role in the world?

- *Faith and Family Life*
  What is the place of self-emptying power in parenting? How might evangelism and mission, as activities of servanthood, be expressed by the family and household?

- *Faith and Involvement*
  Is it possible in the real world of public service for Christians to adopt a self-emptying approach to power, and yet to have a positive influence? What are the implications of this for those whose job or voluntary role includes the exercising of political power?

- *Faith and Working Life*
  How does a Christian view of power impact the dynamics of the workplace? Is it possible or realistic to expect Christians in positions of leadership and authority in the workplace to adopt a self-emptying attitude to their use of power?

Day 5

Voices in Exile:
Turning the cross around

Consider the words of the distinguished Jewish theologian Ignaz Maybaum in a collection of sermons, lectures and essays published under the title *The Face of God After Auschwitz*. ...

The Cross did not prevent the greatest carnage of history from happening; what happened, happened while the Cross was the sign of respectability, while the Star of David was the sign of the outcast; the Cross was the smug symbol of a religion that lived in concordat with Hitler.

... Members of non-Christian religious traditions have often shown awareness that the use of the symbol of the cross in ways like those just described is a perversion of the gospel and a misrepresentation of Jesus Christ. The Jewish novelist Andre Schwarz-Bart seems to have recognised that such an ideological use of the cross involved a fundamental departure from the gospel. Indeed, so radical was the subversion of the original meaning of Christ as to suggest a demonic influence at work within Christendom. In *The Last of the Just* he depicts a Jewish couple walking illegally through German-occupied Paris without their identifying Star of David, discussing the enigma of Christian hatred toward them and their kindred:

'Oh Ernie', Golda said, 'You know them: tell me why, why the Christians hate us the way they do. They seem nice enough when you can look at them without a star.'

Ernie put his arm around her shoulders solemnly. 'It's very mysterious', he murmured in Yiddish, 'They don't exactly know why themselves. I've been in their churches and read their gospels. Do you know who the Christ was? A simple Jew like your father, a kind of *Hasid*'.

Golda smiled gently: 'You're laughing at me'.

'No, no, believe me, and I bet they would have got on very well the two of them, because he was a really good Jew you know, sort of like the *Baal Shem Tov:* a merciful man, and gentle. The Christians say they love him, but I think they hate him without knowing it; so they take the cross by the other end and make a sword out of it, and strike us with it! You understand, Golda,' he cried, suddenly and strangely excited, 'they take the cross and turn it round, they turn it round, my God....'

What this quotation makes clear is that the true meaning of the Christian message, centred on the crucified Messiah, has often been completely obscured and subverted in the actual experience of people in other traditions in contact with the historical phenomenon of the Christian religion.[183]

Voices in Exile:
Castrating culture

(In a moving and well-researched exploration of the place of ethnic minorities in history and in the world today, Dewi Hughes, theological advisor to Tearfund, notes how often in history indigenous peoples have been the victims of a negative conception of power – and how often this has been associated with the Christian churches. His title *Castrating Culture: A Christian Perspective on Ethnic Identity from the Margins* is derived from a statement of Artidoro Tuanama, director of the Association of Quechua Evangelical Churches of the Jungle, in northeastern

Peru: "We simply want to take our place as indigenous and native Quechua people, understanding and living out the gospel. We assume our identity without shame, retaliation or indignation against those who have caused harm to our past and castrated our culture."

Dewi Hughes explains his own struggle in deciding to use such language in the title of his book.)

I hesitated for a long time before deciding

to use 'castrating' in the title, because it is certainly not a nice word and I was afraid of offending Christian sensibilities. It expresses so well, however, the sort of violence that has been done to less powerful *ethnies* that I eventually decided to risk it. I also feel strongly that if Artidoro, who has suffered much and has witnessed the suffering of his people, could use the term to express what has been done to his people, then I should not question his wisdom. I want Christians who belong to the powerful *ethnies* to hear Artidoro.

... His people continue to live most of their lives outside the boundaries of industrialisation and globalisation. They are not numerous. In global terms, and relative to the numerous and powerful nations of the earth, they count for nothing. A very sophisticated electronic scale would be required to even register their existence – for all the great nations of the earth, with their splendour, glory and power, are but dust on God's scales. Before God, the might and longevity of all the nations appear as nothing [Isa 40:15–17].

This may be so, but Artidoro has also understood something of the genius of the gospel with its revelation of a God who 'has brought down rulers from their thrones but has lifted up the humble ... has filled the hungry with good things but has sent the rich away empty' [Luke 1:52–53]. He has understood that, having welcomed the gospel, his little people by the world's standards have a responsibility to live out the gospel in the context of their history and culture. Sadly, that history and culture has been harmed and castrated.

... One of the most devastating effects of ethnic oppression is to make people ashamed of who they are to the point that they try not to be who they are and adopt the identity of their oppressors. Artidoro believes that the gospel, as a glorious manifestation of God's love to him and his people, frees them inwardly from oppression. Any object of God's love cannot be worthless. Therefore, they can be who they are without shame and, in Christ's strength; they can do so without being angry, or wanting to hit back, at their oppressors.[184]

Teaching Block 3:
Power to Thrive: a faithful God for the long haul of a faithful life

3.1 Commitment: clinging to the invisible God

3.2 Confidence: obedient involvement

3.3 Community: foreigners, sojourners and party people

3.4 Connections: the ordinary made extraordinary

3.5 Creativity: re-pitching the tent

The third contrast offered by these confrontations between Daniel and the Babylonian kings is one of perspective: between the short-term goal of vindication and victory and the long-term goal of a faithful life. The danger in reading the power encounters of Daniel is that we will assume that life is always like this, and as a result have a distorted view of the workings of God's power and of the call to faith. The book of Daniel is a selective text, describing only certain incidents in the prophet's long and fruitful life. Gaps of weeks, months, years and even decades are glossed over in the text, while intricate details are given of single incidents

lasting little more than a day. We could be forgiven for assuming that on a daily basis Daniel confronted the awesome power of the emperor, faced death and tested the power of God in a dramatic public showdown. But as far as the narrative is concerned, he didn't. He lived for long periods of 'in-between' time, when the power of God was given, we can assume, not for spectacular vindications but for ordinary life.

What the structure of the book does help us to do is to assess the character of Daniel through these in-between times. The stories of Daniel 1–6 may not be the full account of a life, but they are its bookends. We see Daniel as a very young man, dragged into exile and searching for a foothold of faith; and we see him 65 years later as an old man, still serving God with integrity and still dreaming of the future God has promised. We can't fill in the gaps in detail, but we can in principle: this is a portrait of a man whose faith sustained him for the long haul.

Daniel answers by his very life the question with which we began our exploration of exile in Psalm 137. The exiled Hebrew temple musicians ask mournfully, How can we sing the Lord's song in a strange land? Unable to find an answer, they abandon their instruments and fall into nostalgic despair. Babylon is too much for them, so they long for the city they have lost – Jerusalem. But Daniel's life takes a different course. Plunged just as deeply as his musician friends into the horror of Babylon, he sings the Lord's song – so clearly and loudly that even kings are changed by it. Daniel proves that it is

possible to know, and in some sense to *be,* the presence of God in an alien culture. He speaks out as a prophetic voice in Babylon. He faces, and overcomes, the pressures of persecution and hostility. He proves the power of God in the ordinary and in the extraordinary. Daniel shows that faith in Yahweh can live through exile unscathed, and even come out stronger for it. In so doing he leaves for generations of Jews and Christians a remarkable legacy.

The key assertion of this epic tale is that its hero did not just survive in Babylon: he thrived there. Daniel is a model of a faith that could so easily have been torn apart by the experience of exile but in fact grew through it. Whatever else the power of God is seen to do in Daniel's life, the overall message is clear: *the power of God is the power to thrive in exile*. Five key aspects of Daniel's lifelong faith emerge from the book: offering a window into the workings of God's power in the long haul of an exile experience.

3.1 Commitment:
clinging to the invisible God

God's power is neither easy nor cheap: it is experienced above all by 'God-chasers' – those committed to *pursuing, finding and holding on* to God no matter what.

"The great crisis of humanity today is that it has lost its sense of the invisible. We have become experts in the visible, particularly in the West. If I were called upon to identify briefly the principal trait of the entire 20th century, I would be unable to find anything more precise and pithy than to repeat again and again, 'Men have forgotten God'. The failings of a human consciousness deprived of its divine dimensions have been a determining factor in all the major crimes of this century." Alexander Solzhenitsyn[191]

We have seen throughout the book of Daniel the strength of his commitment to a life of personal discipleship. From his decision, in his youth, to adopt a voluntarily restricted diet (Dan 1) to the evidence, in his old age, of a commitment to regular daily prayer (Dan 6), Daniel comes across as an individual committed to pursuing a life of personal discipline and growth. Daniel's

faith in exile is famous because it is expressed in a public stand: but it is rooted, first and foremost, in a private devotional life.

"Daniel and his friends ... were fully immersed in a pagan culture. They worked hard and succeeded in society. But they did not compromise their religious principles. They challenge the position of those who say it is impossible to be totally committed to God and his principles in a fallen world." Ajith Fernando[185]

It is deep people who survive in difficult times: a faith that thrives in the exile of the twenty-first century will be a faith *grounded in pursuing and knowing God*.

3.2 Confidence:
obedient involvement

God's long-haul power is not revealed to those who hide from the world, or from adversity, but to those willing to *engage* in an environment of exile.

"Without Christ not one step. With him anywhere." David Livingstone[192]

In his relationship to his context and culture, we have seen a keynote of *confidence* in the way in which Daniel conducts himself. His relationship to the wider culture is not arrogant, but neither is it apologetic: he presents his faith in Yahweh as a viable and entirely reasonable alternative to the culturally dominant belief in the gods of Babylon. Ajith Fernando sums up this confidence in terms of three approaches that Christians have tended to take towards the culture in which they find themselves.

- The first is *isolation*, in which Christians keep their distance from a society that is evil and against God's kingdom, preferring instead to 'just survive and do church work'.

- The second response is one of *accommodation*, in which Christians, especially in a minority context, feel that if they are going to succeed in society, they must do so by accommodating themselves to their culture's norms – breaking biblical principles if they need to.

- The third response, the one pursued by Daniel and his friends, is that of *obedient involvement*, in which Christians go into the world with a confidence born out of their belief that God is its creator. "By their life and witness they challenge the wisdom of the world when it opposes God's wisdom, and they demonstrate that God's way is indeed the best way."[186]

Confidence born out of belief empowers those who might otherwise cower in fear to engage boldly with the idols and idolatry of their age. The faith that thrives in the exile of the twenty-first century will be a faith that is *fully and resiliently engaged* with the culture in which it is set.

3.3 Community:
foreigners, sojourners and party people

God's power is not designed for solo operators: it is received, explored, employed and expressed in the formation of mission-focussed communities.

"Perhaps Western culture is nearing a point where the Christian faith can be successfully reintroduced. Maybe the collapse of the present order will lead to a new outbreak of revolutionary Christianity." Howard Snyder[193]

We have also seen the important thread of community that runs through the book of Daniel. Daniel works hard to engage and involve his fellow exiles, and it is as a group that they find strength in exile. In our own time and culture, this same vision of a community of faith 'embracing exile' and sent out to make a difference to the world is captured in more contemporary language by Pete Greig, founder of the fast-growing 24-7 prayer movement.

"Just as 2000 years ago Jesus spent his time at parties, among the crowds, engaging with the disreputable and apparently non-religious, so today he seems surprisingly comfortable among the crowds of party-goers, the non-religious pilgrims of our time. Perhaps he longs for us to vacate our buildings from time to time, to turn our temples into tabernacles, to become like him, the Friend of Sinners. We are the light of the world, but no one wants to stare at the bulb. We are the salt of the earth, but a whole plate of the stuff will make you sick. The people of God are called to scatter and mix, to mingle and move, to influence from a position of weakness, like a small child in a large family, like yeast in a loaf, like a mustard seed beneath a path. Could it be that the Holy Spirit is weary of attending our meetings, and hungers for our presence at his? Perhaps he's dreaming up a thousand new meeting places, where new sounds and sights

burn the eyes and break the heart. Maybe the time has finally come when it will no longer be possible to encounter the fullness of God in Christian conferences and classic meetings. Maybe this is a new day in which the fullness of God awaits us in the streets and clubs and pubs... We've spent 30 years saying 'Come Holy Spirit' and he came. Now, if the Spirit says 'Come', the question is this: will we obey?" Pete Greig and Dave Roberts[187]

Though we often think of Daniel as a 'lone operator', behind the scenes he lived in radical and mutual dependence on his friends and fellow-exiles. People who are prepared to band together most make an impact on their pagan surroundings: the faith that thrives in the exile of the twenty-first century will be a faith *expressed in the shared life* of radical community.

3.4 Connections:
the ordinary made extraordinary

The currents of God's power are strongest where it is *earthed* – touching people who need access to it *through* people who have access to it.

"The way of Christian witness is ... the way of being in Christ, in the Spirit, at the place where the world is in pain, so that the healing love of God may be brought to bear at that point." Tom Wright

A significant element in the story of Daniel is his ability to discern and respond to the connections God gives him in his culture. Though connection to God is clearly his priority, he is never cut off from those around him. Whether dealing with a guard set to watch over him, with a soldier sent to kill him or with the emperor himself, Daniel establishes relationships of impact and influence. Through God-given connections, he finds opportunities in exile to express his faith.

"Almost by definition, the acts of grace that most change the world consist of those actions that will never be widely publicized. They are the stories of the changed lives of very ordinary people. No matter where in the

world you look, those who have become Christians have overwhelmingly made such a decision because of the actions of ordinary people in their circle of influence. These ordinary people are not going to influence the lives of thousands: but there are some individuals with whom they have a particular connection who may listen to no-one else. In a very particular and unique way, they are strategically positioned in relation to some people. It is when the church is able to mobilise the large majority of its membership such that these participants begin to see their lives as unique receivers and givers of grace that the church begins to take on the character of that which it has been called by God to be. It is the ordinary made extraordinary by virtue of a connection to the grace of God." Martin Robertson and Dwight Smith[188]

The kingdom is 'carried' by those who are able to see and respond to the connections God is giving them. The faith that thrives in the exile of the twenty-first century will be a faith *open to God-given connections* with the people it encounters in everyday life.

3.5 Creativity:
re-pitching the tent

The power of God is rarely revealed in lifeless conformity and dull compliance. Faithful to God's character and record, it flows in newness, innovation, creativity and regeneration.

"A church that pitches its tents without constantly looking out for new horizons, that does not continually strike camp, is being

untrue to its calling. ... We must play down our longing for certainty, accept what is risky, live by improvisation and experiment." Hans Kung

Daniel demonstrates a very real *creativity* in the way he deals with the experience of exile. His early 'food fast' is an example of an innovative and unexpected response to difficult circumstances. Through it he and his friends are able to retain their integrity, to maintain a focussed and disciplined faith and to win the affirmation and admiration of their pagan colleagues and masters. This same creativity – often finding surprising ways both to maintain and to express faith – becomes a mark of Daniel's long and accomplished career.

"The central question to be faced is how we should respond to the emerging culture in a way which is true to the gospel. ... It is through risk and experiment together with

the making of mistakes that the future shape of the church in mission will be established."
Graham Cray[189]

Daniel's creative responses to the new and untested circumstances of exile might be described as 'faithful improvisation': he was flexible, adaptable and innovative in meeting new challenges, and yet entirely faithful to his roots as a servant of Yahweh. The faith that thrives in the exile of the twenty-first century will be a faith that is *both rooted and renewed* – true to its past but open to its future.

In The Zone

Consider the challenge to commitment, community, confidence, connections and creativity in the Zone you are exploring. What practical strategies can be drawn from the Daniel story for believers seeking to *thrive* in this area of life?

- *Faith and a Changing World*
  What new *connections* might be available to you in your changing context? What might a response of *creativity* look like in twenty-first century Christian mission?

- *Faith and the Developing World*
  How does the issue of *confidence* relate to those in a non-Western context? How does the call to Christian *community* impact the cultural diversity of God's global family?

- *Faith and Devotional Life*
  What does the call for *commitment* to a dynamic personal spirituality mean for us in the twenty-first century exilic experience? What strategies will be effective in pursuing prayer in today's culture?

- *Faith and Everyday Life*
  What new strategies might be open to you in responding to a changing culture and context? How does the example of Daniel speak to your own situation?

- *Faith and Family Life*
  What are the implications of these five strategic areas to family life? What *connections* are possible in the context of family? How does the call for *creativity* impact the ways in which we function in our communities and neighbourhoods?

- *Faith and Involvement*
  How does the call for *confidence* in terms of obedient involvement translate into our contemporary political context? Does the call to build radical Christian communities militate against involvement in the wider community?

- *Faith and Working Life*
  How might these strategies be worked out and expressed in the context of the working life? Is there a role for Christian *communities* planted directly into the workplace? How can *connections* made through working life become opportunities for faith to be expressed?

Day 5

Question Time

This teaching block suggests that thriving in exile calls for commitment, connections, community, confidence and creativity.

- Which of these areas comes across to you as the most urgent in your own experience of exile?

- In which of these areas do you most need to see growth?

- What strategies, ideas and resources can you identify for your own long-haul journey?

Conclusion:
Faith transforms the experience of exile

The very final 'book-end' in the life of Daniel, given in the last words of the book, are a remarkable key to the understanding of a long-haul faith. After the stories of trial and triumph; after the long life of faithful service; after the dreams and visions of a future in which the sovereign God wins all, Daniel is told by an angel quite simply to *get on with his life*.

"As for you, go your way till the end. You will rest, and then at the end of the days you will rise to receive your allotted inheritance." (Dan 12:13)

Eugene Peterson's translation of the Bible paraphrases the angel's words.

"And you? Go about your business without fretting or worrying. Relax. When it's all over, you will be on your feet to receive your reward." (Dan 12:13, The Message)

The promise is of a future kingdom – a future resurrection. There is an inheritance to come, but the immediate call is to perseverance and faith: 'go your way till the end' or 'go about your business'. An old man, perhaps tired of waiting for the fulfilment of the dreams his God has given him, Daniel is sent, in effect, back into exile. It is in the 'here and now' reality of

Babylon that he must press on to the very end. Deliverance is promised, but the promise is not yet delivered. This parallels the conversation between Jesus and the disciples that we referred to at the very outset of our exploration of Daniel. Just as the angel calls Daniel to faithful witness, so Jesus offers to his disciples both the certainty of the kingdom that is coming and the challenge of the life that must be lived until it comes.

"It is not for you to know the times or dates the Father has set by his own authority. But you will receive power when the Holy Spirit comes on you; and you will be my witnesses in Jerusalem, and in all Judea and Samaria, and to the ends of the earth." (Acts 1:7,8)

You *will* receive power, and you *will* be his witnesses: but it will be in the here and now, in exile, in all the places to which his Spirit sends you. The kingdom of God is promised: the sovereignty of God in history guarantees it. There is a day coming when exile and alienation, trauma and trial will be no more. But that is the *not yet* of God's kingdom. The *now* is a world waiting for the touch of God's grace; a world deep in thrall to false gods; deep in the darkness of injustice. The *now* is Babylon. The power of God is given for your exile.

Voices in Exile:
The Godbearing life

In 1980, eight-year-old Andy Bremner was diagnosed with cancer. During his first hospitalisation, he received a deluge of cards and letters from his classmates and his Scout troupe. Letters poured in for five days – and then they stopped. His mother, Linda, noticed that in that brief span of time those letters had become a kind of lifeline for Andy, so she decided to pick up the slack quietly. Every few days she sent him a note, signing it "Your Secret Pal".

She didn't think Andy suspected anything. Then one day she found her son sketching at the kitchen table. He wouldn't let her see what he was drawing. "It's for my secret pal," he explained. After Andy fell asleep, Linda sneaked a peek at the picture he had drawn for his secret pal. What she found drove an arrow through her heart: a child's picture and below it the words: "I love you mommy".

For the next four years, Linda Bremner wrote to her son. When he died in 1984, she found every letter she had written him stashed like treasure in the back of his closet, along with an address book from a camp he had attended for children with cancer. Linda kept the address book, and one by one she wrote to every child listed there. The response was enormous. "Thank you, thank you, thank you", one child wrote back: "I didn't know anybody knew that I *lived*."

Linda posted a sign-up sheet at Children's Hospital in Chicago, where Andy had been treated, for terminally ill children who might like a secret pal. She was inundated with names. When writing to each child became too much for her to handle alone, she enlisted the help of her family. As more and more names poured in, to meet the demand Linda eventually founded Love Letters, a Chicago-based non-profit organisation now staffed by sixty-five volunteers who write 1,100 notes every week to children they have never met.

That story kept pestering me until I did something about it. I called Linda Bremner to get some more information. I asked her what gave her the fortitude for such an undertaking, still going strong fourteen years after Andy's death. "We don't call it a ministry," she said. "But that's what it is. Society has taught us that touch – physical or emotional – is dangerous, and I understand the concern. But we're out to touch people."

What kind of logic could explain the brazen courage, the inner strength that voluntarily relives the death of your own child day after day through the names of other terminally ill children whose stories flood your office? On the other hand, isn't that what God does for us? It's not logical that God can take the inexplicable death of a twelve-year-old boy and use it to bring hope to more than a thousand children every week. It's not logical that God can take people who never imagined themselves ministers and use them to deliver 'love letters' from God, however unwittingly, to people desperate for a touch of transformation. It's not logical that God can use unlikely people like Mary and Moses, ordinary people like you and I, to bear Christ's love to the world again and again. But then nobody becomes a Godbearer out of logic. We are Godbearers because two thousand years ago in a stable in Bethlehem, God delivered a love letter addressed to us.[190]

Day 5

Voices in Exile:
Books to read in Babylon

Against the Stream: Christianity and Mission in an age of Globalisation (IVP, 2003) is David Smith's follow-up to his important treatment of *Mission After Christendom*. In *Against the Stream* he explores the place of Christianity in a world in which the West no longer dominates. How does the Christian faith now face up to the world's other religious systems? And is there a need for Christianity itself to be liberated from the distortions and encumbrances brought about by its long partnership with Western progress? With new and often challenging insights, this is an important book for all those concerned for the future of global Christian mission.

Jim Cymbala's **Fresh Power** (*Zondervan, 2003*) is the latest instalment in the story of the remarkable Brooklyn Tabernacle in New York. Representing a fairly 'classical' Pentecostal theology, Cymbala calls for a radical dependence in church life on prayer and on the power of the Holy Spirit. The book is particularly uplifting in its stories of individuals transformed by God's power. These include drug addicts and hardened criminals and, most movingly, David Berkowitz; the notorious 'Son of Sam' serial killer who is still serving out a jail term running to hundreds of years.

Captain America and the Crusade against Evil: The Dilemma of Zealous Nationalism (*Eerdmans, 2003*) by Robert Jewett and John Shelton Lawrence is an analysis by two American professors of theology of their own government's recent foreign policy. Relying both on biblical sources and on a comprehensive analysis of the history of 'zealous nationalism', Jewett and Lawrence call for an urgent re-discovery of the possibilities of 'redemptive love'. Aimed at an academic readership, this book is an important contribution to the understanding of faith and politics in the contemporary world, and an application of biblical principles to a specific example of political force.

Canon John Holmes' essay **Vulnerable Evangelism: The Way of Jesus** (Grove Booklets) is a brief but very helpful exploration of the impact of 'servant leadership' on the practice of evangelism. An Anglo-Catholic with significant experience of mission in a parish setting, the author is particularly keen to see local churches empowered as servant-evangelists in their communities.

Chris Edmondson carries a heartfelt concern for the training, development and health of church leaders for the twenty-first century. **Fit to Lead: Sustaining Effective Ministry in a Changing World** (*Darton, Longman and Todd, 2002*) takes a serious look at the changes sweeping through our culture and at the needs of the church and of its leaders. Written in a down-to-earth and accessible style *Fit to Lead* is honest about the pressures leaders face and offers practical, workable and morale-boosting resources for change and growth. Recommended for all those in leadership, in training for leadership or considering a leadership role.

Castrating Culture: A Christian Perspective on Ethnic Identity from the Margins (*Paternoster, 2002*) is Dewi Hughes' passionate and personal exploration of the place of ethnic minorities in the world, and in God's plan. Hughes reflects both on his exposure, through Tearfund, to ethnic issues on a global scale and on his own experience, closer to home, in the uneasy relationship between his Welsh-speaking community and their English neighbours. A provocative and challenging book that speaks with genuine authority into a complex and important issue.

(Endnotes)

1 John Holdsworth, *Dwelling in a Strange Land: Exile in the Bible and in the Church* (Canterbury Press, 2003) p13

2 Stephen Travis, *The Bible as a Whole* (The Bible Reading Fellowship, 1994) p199

3 Tremper Longman III, *The NIV Application Commentary: Daniel* (Zondervan, 1999) p21

4 *Expositor's Bible Commentary, Old Testament,* (Zondervan, 1992)

5 John Goldingay, *Word Biblical Commentary: Daniel* (Word, 1989) pxl

6 Longman, *NIV Application Commentary*, p57

7 Holdsworth, *Dwelling in a Strange Land,* p19

8 Geoff Dyer, cited in Pico Iyer, *The Global Soul: Jet-Lag, Shopping Malls and the Search for Home* (London: Bloomsbury, 2000) p79

9 Ronald Rolheiser, *Forgotten Among the Lilies: Learning to Live Beyond Our Obsessions* (Hodder and Stoughton, 1990) p13

10 Rob Lacey, *The Street Bible* (Zondervan, 2002)

11 Goldingay, *Daniel,* p21

12 Ibid., p22

13 Viv Thomas, *Second Choice: Embracing Life As It Is* (Carlisle: Paternoster, 2000) p3

14 Ibid., p5,13

15 Goldingay, *Daniel,* p21

16 Thomas, *Second Choice,* p119

17 Cited in Pico Iyer, *The Global Soul,* p116

18 Thomas, *Second Choice,* p95

19 Walter Brueggemann, *Hopeful Imagination: Prophetic Voices from Exile* (Philadelphia: Fortress Press, 1986) p1

20 Ibid., p4

21 Cited in Pico Iyer, *The Global Soul,* p37

22 Peter Phillips, *I Peter as Rhetorical Liturgy* (Cliff College, 2004)

23 Ernest Lucas, editorial comment (October 2004)

24 Tim Chester & Steve Timmis, 'The Principles of Gospel Ministry' in *The Briefing,* Issue 234 (April 21, 2000), p.6

25 Callum Brown, *The Death of Christian Britain* (Routledge, 2001) p1

26 Robert Jensen, cited in Stuart Murray, *Post-Christendom: Church and Mission in a Strange New World* (Paternoster, 2004) p18

27 James D Berkley, *Essential Christianity: Finding the God Who Loves You* (Zondervan, 2001) p10

28 David Smith, *Mission After Christendom* (Darton, Longman and Todd, 2003) p35

29 Michael Frost and Alan Hirsch, *The Shaping of Things to Come* (Hendrickson Publishers, Inc., 2003)

30 Stuart Murray, *Post-Christendom: Church and Mission in a Strange New World* (Paternoster, 2004) p110

31 Graham Cray, *Youth Congregations and the Emerging Church* (Grove Books, 2002)

32 Cited in Murray, *Post-Christendom,* p287

33 Grace Davie, *Europe: The Exceptional Case – Parameters of Faith in the Modern World* (Darton, Longman and Todd, 2002) pxi

34 Murray, *Post-Christendom,* p6

35 Brown, *Death of Christian Britain,* cited in Murray, *Post-Christendom,* p5

36 John and Olive Drane, cited in Murray, *Post-Christendom,* p7

37 Kenneth Leech, *Through Our Long Exile: Contextual Theology and the Urban Experience* (Darton, Longman and Todd, 2001) p229

38 *Expositor's Bible Commentary, Old Testament* (Zondervan, 1992)

39 Wilbert R. Shenk, *Changing Frontiers of Mission* (Orbis Books, 1999) p183

40 Pete Ward, *Liquid Church* (Paternoster, 2002) p3

41 Robert Wuthnow, *Loose Connections: Joining Together in America's Fragmented Communities* (Harvard University Press, 1998) p2

42 Ibid., p2

43 Murray, *Post-Christendom,* p20

44 John R W Stott, The Bible Speaks Today: *The Message of Ephesians* (Inter-Varsity Press, 1979) p135

45 Frost and Hirsch, *The Shaping of Things to Come*

46 Smith, *Mission After Christendom,* p35

47 Eugene Peterson, *Introduction to the Prophets*, The Message

48 Ernest Lucas, editorial comment (October 2004)

49 Longman, *NIV Application Commentary*, p84

50 Ernest C. Lucas, *Apollos Old Testament Commentary: Daniel* (Apollos/Inter-Varsity Press, 2002) p78

51 Graham Tomlin, *The Provocative Church* (SPCK, 2002) p127

52 Goldingay, Daniel

53 Peterson, The Message

54 Walter Brueggemann, *Finally Comes the Poet: Daring Speech for Proclamation* (Fortress Press, 1989) p4

55 Longman, *NIV Application Commentary*, p 228

56 Craig Bartholomew, 'Consuming God's Word: Biblical Interpretation and Consumerism', in *Christ and Consumerism: A Critical Analysis of the Spirit of the Age*, Craig Bartholomew and Thorsten Moritz eds. (Paternoster, 2000) p89

57 Graham McFarlane, 'God, Self and Society: Variations on a Trinitarian Theme', in *Movement for Change: Evangelical Perspectives on Social Transformation*, David Hilborn ed. (Paternoster, 2004) p64

58 P D Kenneson and J L Street, *Selling Out the Church: The Dangers of Church Marketing* (Nashville: Abingdon, 1997) p23

59 Jurgen Moltmann, *The Church in the Power of the Spirit*, cited in Roy McCloughry, *Living in the Presence of the Future* (Inter-Varsity Press, 2001) p166

60 Tomlin, *The Provocative Church,* p61

61 Ibid., p22,156

62 Walter Brueggemann, *Biblical Perspectives on Evangelism: Living in a Three-Storied Universe* (Abingdon Press, 1993) p14

63 Acts 2:12; Amazed and perplexed, they asked one another, "What does this mean?"

64 Smith, *Mission After Christendom*, p90

65 Longman, *NIV Application Commentary*, p177

66 Kathy Galloway, 'Singing the Lord's Song', in *Worship for Housing Estate Ministry: Singing the Lord's Song in a Strange Land* (National Estate Churches Network, 2003) p7

67 Roy McCloughry, *Living in the Presence of the Future* (Inter-Varsity Press, 2001) p128

68 Longman, *NIV Application Commentary*, p141

69 Galloway, 'Singing the Lord's Song', p15

70 McCloughry, *Living in the Presence of the Future*, p18

71 Bartholomew *Consuming God's Word*, p93

72 Peterson, *The Message*

73 Bartholomew *Consuming God's Word*, p92

74 Leonardo Boff, Cited in Graham McFarlane, 'God, Self and Society: Variations on a Trinitarian Theme', in *Movement for Change: Evangelical Perspectives on Social Transformation*, David Hilborn ed. (Paternoster, 2004) p65

75 Smith, *Mission After Christendom*, p44

76 Jim Wallis, 'Christian Values and the Three Poverties', The Second Temple Address, 2002, published in *Movement for Change*, Hilborn ed., p164

77 Steve Chalke *Faithworks: Intimacy and Involvement*

78 Joel Edwards Evangelical Alliance, 2004

79 David Bebbington, 'Evangelicals, Theology and Social Transformation', in *Movement for Change*, Hilborn ed , p10

80 Ajith Fernando, *Spiritual Living in a Secular World: Applying the Book of Daniel Today* (Monarch Books, 2002)

81 The Micah Declaration on Integral Mission, http://www.micahnetwork.org

82 Joe Kapolyo, 'Social Transformation as a Missional Imperative', in *Movement for Change*, Hilborn ed., p139

83 Wallis, 'Christian Values', p155

84 Tim Chester, *Good News to the Poor: Sharing the Gospel Through Social Involvement* (Inter-Varsity Press, 2004) p132

85 Tomlin, *The Provocative Church*, p123

86 Hans Urs von Balthasar, cited in Walter Brueggemann, *Finally Comes the Poet: Daring Speech for Proclamation* (Fortress Press, 1989) p4

87 Brueggemann, *Finally Comes the Poet*, p3

88 Ibid., p123

89 Ibid., p6

90 Smith, *Mission After Christendom*, p34

91 Brueggemann, *Hopeful Imagination*, p41

92 Walter Brueggemann, *The Prophetic Imagination* (Fortress Press, 1978) p45

93 Longman, *NIV Application Commentary*, p178

94 Ernest Lucas editorial comment, October 2004, see also Ernest Lucas, *Decoding Daniel: Reclaiming the Visions of Daniel 7-11* (Grove Books, 2000)

95 Thomas Merton, *Praying the Psalms* (Liturgical Press, 1956) p7

96 Henri Nouwen, *The Genesee Diary: Report from a Trappist Monastery* (Doubleday, 1976) entry under Friday, August 2nd

97 Brueggemann, *Finally Comes the Poet*, p142

98 Brueggemann, *Hopeful Imagination*, p26, 97

99 Conrad Gempf, *Jesus Asked: What He Wanted to Know* (Zondervan, 2003) p25

100 Brian D. McLaren, *The Church on the Other Side: Doing Ministry in the Postmodern Matrix* (Zondervan, 2000) p89

101 Brueggemann, *Hopeful Imagination*, p130

102 Copyright © Gerard Kelly, 2002

103 McLaren, *The Church on the Other Side*, p73-74

104 Goldingay, *Daniel*, p72

105 Ibid., p76

106 Ibid., p133

107 Longman, *NIV Application Commentary*, p167

108 Ibid., p168

109 Lacey, *Street Bible*

110 Holdsworth, *Dwelling in a Strange Land*, p24

111 George Everett Ross, cited in Philip Yancey, *Reaching for the Invisible God: What Can we Expect to Find?* (Zondervan, 2000) p52

112 Longman, *NIV Application Commentary*, p264

113 Dr Gordon Temple, Chief Executive, Torch Trust for the Blind

114 Yancey, *Reaching for the Invisible God*, p53

115 Anna Lee Stangl, *Tried by Fire: Testimonies of Courage and Hope from Peru's Christian Prisoners* (Monarch, 2003) Preface

117 Stangl, *Tried by Fire*, Preface

118 Richard Wurmbrand, *Tortured for Christ* (Living Sacrifice Book Company, 1967, 1998) pp34,35,37

119 Ibid., p150

120 Nelson Mandela, *Long Walk to Freedom* (Abacus, 1995) p171

121 Tertullian, *Apology 50*, cited in Tony Lane, *The Lion Concise Handbook of Christian Thought* (Lion, 1984) p16

122 Martin Luther King Jr., *Strength to Love* (Fontana Religious, 1963) p54

123 Wurmbrand, *Tortured for Christ*, p52,55

124 Ibid., p63

125 Dan Bauman, *Imprisoned in Iran: Love's Victory over Fear* (YWAM Publishing, 2000) p122-123

126 Ian Coffey, *Doorways from the Word to the World* (Bible Reading Fellowship, 2003) p48

127 Daniel I Block, *The Gods of the Nations: Studies in Ancient Near-Eastern National Theology* (Grand Rapids: Baker Academic, 2000) p62

128 Ibid., p70

129 Pete Lowman, *A Long Way East of Eden: Could God Explain the Mess We're in?* (Paternoster, 2002) p257

130 Longman, *NIV Application Commentary*, p109

131 Joel Edwards, Evangelical Alliance, 2004

132 Brueggemann, *Finally Comes the Poet*, p121

133 Ibid., p121

134 Doug Barnett, editorial comment, October 2004

135 Lucas, *Apollos Old Testament Commentary*, p154

136 Bill Hybels, *Too Busy Not to Pray: Slowing Down to be with God* (Inter-Varsity Press, 1988) p99

137 Cited in Yancey, *Reaching for the Invisible God*, p208

138 Richard Foster, *Prayer: Finding the Heart's True Home* (Hodder and Stoughton, 1992)

139 Steve McVey, *The Divine Invitation* (Harvest House, 2002) p140, cited in Tony Horsfall, *Rhythms of Grace: Finding Intimacy with God in a Busy Life* (Kingsway, 2004) p29

140 Roy Lawrence, *How to Pray When Life Hurts* (Scripture Union, 1993, 2003) p39

141 R. Paul Stevens, *Down to Earth Spirituality: Encountering God in the Ordinary, Boring Stuff of Life* (Inter-Varsity Press, 2003) p13

142 *Carmina Gadelica, I, p.63,* cited in Esther De Waal, *The Celtic Way of Prayer: The Recovery of the Religious Imagination* (Hodder and Stoughton, 1996) p72

143 Kenda Creasy Dean and Ron Foster, *The Godbearing Life: the Art of Soul Tending for Youth Ministry* (Upper Room Books, 1998) p169

144 Lawrence, *How to Pray When Life Hurts*, p28

145 Rowan Williams, Archbishop of Canterbury, *Enthronement Sermon* (Canterbury Cathedral, 2003)

146 Copyright © Gerard Kelly, 2003

147 Sokreaksa S. Himm, *The Tears of my Soul* (Monarch, 2003) p117, 127

148 Hybels, *Too Busy Not to Pray*, p150

149 Longman, *NIV Application Commentary*, p168,169

150 Brueggemann, *The Prophetic Imagination*, p112

151 H. G. Wells, *History of the World* (Middlesex: Pelican, 1960) p157, cited in Alan Storkey, *The Politics of Jesus* (2004)

152 Longman, *NIV Application Commentary*, p129

153 Brueggemann, *Finally Comes the Poet*, p126

154 Longman, *NIV Application Commentary*, p145

155 Ibid., p137

156 Ibid., p141

157 Lucas, Apollos Old Testament Commentary, p137

158 Ibid., p114

159 Hybels, *Too Busy Not to Pray*, p13

160 D. L. Moody, cited in Jim Cymbala, *Fresh Power* (Zondervan, 2001) p8

161 Cymbala, *Fresh Power*, p14

162 Samuel Escobar, *A Time for Mission: The Challenge for Global Christianity* (Inter-Varsity Press, 2003) p175

163 Justo J. Gonzales, *For the Healing of the Nations: The Book of Revelation in an Age of Cultural Conflict* (Orbis Books, 1999) p91, cited in Smith, *Mission After Christendom,* p110

164 Cited in Dewi Hughes, *Castrating Culture: A Christian Perspective on Ethnic Identity from the Margins* (Paternoster, 2001) p170

165 Brueggemann, *Finally Comes the Poet*, p131

166 Robert Jewett and John Shelton Lawrence, *Captain America and the Crusade Against Evil: The Dilemma of Zealous Nationalism* (Eerdmans, 2003) p271

167 Longman, *NIV Application Commentary*, p170, 171

168 Brueggemann, *The Prophetic Imagination*, p95

169 Alan Storkey, *The Politics of Jesus,* (2004)

170 Jewett and Lawrence, *Captain America and the Crusade Against Evil*, p271

171 Bamber Gascoigne, *The Christians* (Book Club Associates, 1977) p16

172 David Bosch, *Transforming Mission* (Orbis, 1991) p193

173 Longman, *NIV Application Commentary*, p303

174 Ian Cowley, *Going Empty Handed: The True Source of Spiritual Power and Authority* (Monarch, 1996) p92

175 Dan Drápal, *Will We Survive Western Missionaries?* (Copyright © Dan Drápal, 1997) p4

176 *Mission and Evangelism – an Ecumenical Affirmation* (World Council of Churches, 1983) cited in John Holmes, *Vulnerable Evangelism: The Way of Jesus* (Grove Books, 2001) p23

177 Storkey, *The Politics of Jesus*

178 Viv Thomas, *Future-Leader* (Paternoster, 1999) p176

179 Rob Bell, Pastor of Mars Hill Bible Church, Grand Rapids, Michigan, cited in Robert Webber, *The Younger Evangelicals: Facing the Challenges of the New World* (Baker Books, 2002) p145

180 Chester, *Good News to the Poor*, p160

181 David Adam, *The Cry of the Deer: Meditation on the Hymn of St. Patrick* (SPCK, 1987) p41

182 David Smith, *Against the Stream: Christianity and Mission in an Age of Globalisation,* (Inter-Varsity Press, 2003) p123

183 Ibid., p117

184 Dewi Hughes, *Castrating Culture: A Christian Perspective on Ethnic Identity from the Margins* (Paternoster, 2001) p221-223

185 Fernando, *Spiritual Living in a Secular World*

186 Ibid.

187 Pete Greig and Dave Roberts, *Red Moon Rising: The Story of 24-7 Prayer* (Survivor, 2003) p230

188 Martin Robinson and Dwight Smith, *Invading Secular Space: Strategies for Tomorrow's Church* (Monarch, 2003) p105

189 Graham Cray in Cray et al, *The Post Evangelical Debate* (London: SPCK, 1997) p2

190 Dean and Foster, *The Godbearing Life*, p208-209

191 Alexander Solzhenitsyn, speech on receiving the 1983 Templeton Prize, cited in Cardinal Cormac Murphy-O'Connor, Archbishop of Westminster, sixth annual Douglas W. Bryant Lecture (12 June, 2001), http://www.rcdow.org.uk/archbishop/010612.htm

192 David Livingstone, http://www.urbana.org/_articles.cfm?RecordId=487

193 Howard Snyder, *The Radical Wesley: Patterns for Church Renewal* (Downers Grove, Ill.: InterVarsity Press, 1980), preface